Trustworthy Policies for Distributed Repositories

Synthesis Lectures on Information Concepts, Retrieval, and Services

Gary Marchionini, *University of North Carolina, Chapel Hill*

Synthesis Lectures on Information Concepts, Retrieval, and Services publishes short books on topics pertaining to information science and applications of technology to information discovery, production, distribution, and management. Potential topics include: data models, indexing theory and algorithms, classification, information architecture, information economics, privacy and identity, scholarly communication, bibliometrics and webometrics, personal information management, human information behavior, digital libraries, archives and preservation, cultural informatics, information retrieval evaluation, data fusion, relevance feedback, recommendation systems, question answering, natural language processing for retrieval, text summarization, multimedia retrieval, multilingual retrieval, and exploratory search.

Automated Metadata in Multimedia Information Systems: Creation, Refinement, Use in Surrogates, and Evaluation
Michael G. Christel

Trustworthy Policies for Distributed Repositories
Reagan W. Moore, Hao Xu, Mike Conway, Arcot Rajasekar, Jon Crabtree, and Helen Tibbo

ISBN: 978-3-031-01175-7 print
ISBN: 978-3-031-02303-3 ebook

DOI 10.1007/978-3-031-02303-3

A Publication in the Morgan & Claypool Publishers series
SYNTHESIS LECTURES ON INFORMATION CONCEPTS, RETRIEVAL, AND SERVICES #51

Series Editor: Gary Marchionini, University of North Carolina, Chapel Hill

Series ISSN 1947-945X Print   1947-9468 Electronic

Trustworthy Policies for Distributed Repositories

Reagan W. Moore, Hao Xu, Mike Conway, Arcot Rajasekar, Jon Crabtree, and Helen Tibbo

DataNet Federation Consortium, University of North Carolina at Chapel Hill

SYNTHESIS LECTURES ON INFORMATION CONCEPTS, RETRIEVAL, AND SERVICES #51

ABSTRACT

A trustworthy repository provides assurance in the form of management documents, event logs, and audit trails that digital objects are being managed correctly. The assurance includes plans for the sustainability of the repository, the accession of digital records, the management of technology evolution, and the mitigation of the risk of data loss. A detailed assessment is provided by the ISO-16363:2012 standard, "Space data and information transfer systems—Audit and certification of trustworthy digital repositories." This book examines whether the ISO specification for trustworthiness can be enforced by computer actionable policies. An implementation of the policies is provided and the policies are sorted into categories for procedures to manage externally generated documents, specify repository parameters, specify preservation metadata attributes, specify audit mechanisms for all preservation actions, specify control of preservation operations, and control preservation properties as technology evolves. An application of the resulting procedures is made to enforce trustworthiness within National Science Foundation data management plans.

KEYWORDS

trustworthiness, long-term preservation, digital repositories, data management, policy, digital preservation, ISO 16363

Contents

Preface

The definition of repository trustworthiness has been under development for more than 10 years. The original specification was created in 2005 by the National Archives and Records Administration (NARA) based on the tasks required for an Electronic Records Archive (ERA) [19]. The list included 852 tasks, of which more than 200 tasks could be automated using policy-based data management systems. In collaboration with the Research Libraries Group, the RLG/NARA Trusted Digital Repository (TDR) criteria [12, 18, 20] were then defined, which reduced the number of necessary computer actionable tasks to about 175. The list was further refined to create the TRAC standard, the Trusted Repository Audit Checklist [21], which included about 120 computer actionable tasks. The tasks were designed to manage systems that complied with the Open Archival Information Systems standard [16].

The repository audit and certification working group [1] for the Mission Operations and Information Management Services (MOIMS) of the Consultative Committee for Space Data (ISO MOIMS-rac) provided additional refinements to the trustworthiness assessment criteria, culminating in the ISO-16363:2012 standard [2, 3, 17]. Trustworthiness criteria are defined for the categories of Organizational Infrastructure, Digital Object Management, and Technical Infrastructure and Risk Management. For each category, explicit tasks are specified that need to be enforced for a repository to be trustworthy. A total of 113 tasks are specified by the ISO standard. A research question is how many of these tasks can be automatically enforced using computer actionable policies.

In this book we analyze the tasks in the ISO 16363 standard. For each category and each task, a set of policies is defined. Computer actionable rules are proposed for automating each task, persistent state attributes are defined that are needed to track the outcome of each task, and example reports are presented for implementing a trustworthy repository. The policies are available on http://github.com under the repository DICE-UNC / policy-workbook / ISO / Rules. This paper defines a minimal set of policies, state information, and operations that are needed to automate tasks required for managing a trustworthy repository.

Acknowledgments

The development of the iRODS data grid was funded by the NSF OCI-1032732 grant, "SDCI Data Improvement: Improvement and Sustainability of iRODS Data Grid Software for Multi-Disciplinary Community Driven Application," (2010–2013). The results presented in this paper were funded by the NSF Cooperative Agreement OCI-094084, "DataNet Federation Consortium," (2011–2016). The iRODS Consortium developed the pluggable architecture used by the DataNet Federation Consortium. The software systems described in this paper are available as open source software on http://github.com.

CHAPTER 1

Introduction

The simplest interpretation of trustworthiness is the preservation of authenticity, integrity, chain of custody, and original arrangement. These are the criteria for preserving paper records at the National Archives and Records Administration. The actual preservation processes that are used depend upon the implementation. For example:

- Authenticity might be maintained through assignment of metadata for the source and provider of each record.

- Integrity might be maintained through use of checksums and replication.

- Chain of custody might be maintained through assignment of access controls and the use of audit trails that track preservation actions.

- Original arrangement might be maintained through administrative metadata that tracks object membership in a record series and the deposition order.

In each case, the repository has to manage state information, maintain links between the state information and the records, and track all actions. The repository must also manage technology evolution. The preservation properties have to be maintained as technology flows through the archives.

1.1 MOTIVATING IMPLEMENTATION PLAN FOR A TRUSTWORTHY REPOSITORY

The ISO 16363 standard provides a set of tasks that ensure the trustworthiness of a repository. The tasks can be organized into a set of activities that should be done to build a trustworthy repository. The tasks include:

Creation of management documents. There are 47 documents that should be generated by the management team, but can be managed within the repository. These documents describe management plans, budgets, sustainability plans, operational procedures, technology assessments, and preservation requirements.

iRODS Name	Report Contents	iRODS Name	Report Contents
Archive-AIP	AIP template for required metadata	Archive-IRL	Technology Risk report
Archive-APU	Audit of Performance	Archive-META	Metadata records for SIPs and AIPs
Archive-AU	Authenticity requirements report	Archive-MS	Mission Statement
Archive-BR	Budget report	Archive-OP	Operations Plan
Archive-BPR	Business Planning report	Archive-PIP	Preservation Implementation Plan (versions)
Archive-CE	ISO 17799 certification	Archive-PL	Technology Change report
Archive-CFR	Confirmation Report	Archive-PSP	Preservation Strategic Plan
Archive-CID	Content Information report	Archive-PR	Security Patch report
Archive-CM	Change Management report	Archive-QAR	Process Verification report
Archive-CollP	Collection Policy	Archive-SAR	Submission Agreement report
Archive-CP	Contingency Plan	Archive-SE	Staff Experience report
Archive-CR	Certification reports	Archive-SIP	SIP template for required metadata
Archive-DAR	Deposit Agreement report (metadata)	Archive-SL	Service Level Agreement report
Archive-DCP	Designated Community	Archive-SOP	Standard Operating Procedure
Archive-DCR	Designated Community Review	Archive-SP	Succession Plan
Archive-DIP	DIP template for required metadata	Archive-SRF	Security Risk Factors
Archive-DD	Disputed Data set report	Archive-SSR	SIP Submission Requirements report
Archive-EAP	Escrow Arrangement plan	Archive-STAR	SIP to AIP Process Description report
Archive-ERR	Error Reports	Archive-STFP	Staffing Plan
Archive-FAR	Financial Audit report	Archive-TAR	Technical audit reports

Archive-FR	Financial Risk report	Archive-TC	Technology/Community report – surveys
Archive-IA	Infrastructure Acquisition report	Archive-TSE	Test System Evaluation Report
Archive-INP	Information Properties report	Archive-TW	Technology Watch report
Archive-IP	Intellectual Property report		

These reports must be versioned, checksummed, replicated, stored in an appropriate collection, and must have an audit date for review. There are an additional five sets of policy specifications that are needed to enforce both the repository attributes and the preservation properties.

Specification of repository parameters. The repository uses static parameters to define control information such as the collection hierarchy for storing digital objects, and default values for the e-mail of the administrator and for the audit review period.

Specification of preservation metadata attributes. The repository specifies the variable names that are used to describe preservation properties such as:

- process control flags;

- process status flags;

- preservation description information;

- representation information for AIPs;

- description information for AIPs; and

- provenance information for AIPs.

Specification of audit mechanisms to track all preservation actions. There are three typical mechanisms for tracking actions or changes to digital objects.

1. Versioning of digital objects on each update

2. Logging of actions in a manifest file

3. Auditing of all actions in an external indexing system

Every action has to be trackable to verify preservation properties. An implication is that every policy or procedure that is applied in the repository has to be logged or audited.

Specification of policies that control operations performed upon the digital objects. Policies can be defined in three different categories.

1. Control interactions with users

2. Control interactions with technology components

3. Control operations performed upon the records

For each category there are three types of policies that are needed.

1. Set default values for control parameters needed for the operation

2. Provide a workflow/procedure to execute the operation

3. Verify the result

Specification of infrastructure that manages technology evolution. A major requirement for a repository is that the records are preserved independently of the choice of technology. Any system components that are chosen today will be replaced at some point in the future. Fortunately data grids are generic infrastructure that manage technology evolution through the use of plug-ins. As each new technology is added to the repository, interactions are controlled through plug-ins that do the required protocol conversions, parameter setting, and operation invocation.

By examining each of the tasks specified by ISO 16363, an implementation of a trustworthy repository can be defined. The selection of the repository parameters, the preservation metadata attributes, the audit mechanisms, and the policies will depend upon the type of records that are being preserved. An example of applying each of these specifications in the construction of a trustworthy repository that satisfies the ISO 16363 trustworthiness criteria is given in Chapter 6.

1.2   NSF DATA MANAGEMENT PLAN EXAMPLE

There are many types of policy sets that can be constructed for data management applications. Examples include collection building for a research project, data sharing for research collaborations, data publication in digital libraries, management of protected data, preservation of data in an archive, and enforcement of National Science Foundation Data Management Plans. A noteworthy result is that for most of these applications, policy sets that enforce ISO 16363 criteria implement appropriate data management processes. The ISO 16363 criteria form a superset of policies that can be used to control multiple types of data management applications.

An example of the application of ISO 16363 policies is the set of requirements for NSF Data Management Plans (DMP). Table 1.1 maps 38 NSF data management plan tasks to equivalent ISO 16363 tasks. For each DMP task the corresponding ISO 16363 task is defined, as well as the associated ISO 16363 report that documents the execution of the task. Note that two of the DMP tasks represent specific preservation metadata requirements. An "instrument type" is needed that can be mapped to the source of a SIP, and a retention policy is needed that can be mapped to a specific record.

Table 1.1: NSF Data Management Plans mapped to ISO 16363			
DMP Tasks	ISO Task	ISO Document	iRODS Document Name
Managers and staff	3.2.1.1	Staffing Plan	Archive-STFP
Costs	3.4.2	Financial Audit report	Archive-FAR
Collection plans	3.1.3	Collection Policy	Archive-CollP
Instrument types	4.1.1	Information Properties report	Archive-INP
Event log	4.2.10	Audit report of all actions	Archive-ARUA
Collection report	4.1.1.2	Content Information Deposition report	Archive-CIRA
Required data policies	3.3.2	Preservation Policies (rule base)	Archive-PPA
Data category	4.1.3	SIP template for required metadata	Archive-SIP
Use of existing data	4.1.1	Source of data	Audit-Source
Quality control	4.2.8	AIP Compliance report	Archive-AIPCRA
Analysis plans	3.2.1	Operations Plan	Archive-OP
Data sharing during analysis	3.5.1.4	Access list	Archive-ALRA
Data dictionary/ glossary	4.3.2.1	HIVE Vocabulary Ontology	Archive-HVOA
Naming	4.1.1	Policy Metadata report	Archive-PMRA
Data format type	4.2.5.4	AIP template for required metadata	Archive-AIP
DOI for data sets	4.2.4.1	Handle Duplicate Audit report	Archive-IDCA
Metadata standard	3.3.1	Designated Community	Archive-DCP
Metadata export method	4.6.2	DIP template for required metadata	Archive-DIP
Collection	4.1.6	Archives Content report	Archive-ARA
Size	4.1.2	Content Information report	Archive-CID
Make original data public	3.5.2	Submission Agreement report	Archive-SAR

Make data products public	3.5.2	Submission Agreement report	Archive-SAR
Re-use	3.5.1.2	Submission Agreement report	Archive-SAR
Re-distribution	3.5.1.2	Submission Agreement report	Archive-SAR
Access restrictions	3.5.1.1	Deposit Agreement report	Archive-DAR
IPR	3.5.2	Intellectual Property report	Archive-IP
Web access	5.1.1	Infrastructure List report	Archive-ILA
Data sharing system	5.1.1	Infrastructure List report	Archive-ILA
Code distribution system	5.1.1	Infrastructure List report	Archive-ILA
Retention period	3.3.2	Preservation Policies	Archive-PPA
Curation	3.3.2	Preservation Policies	Archive-PPA
Archive	3.3.2	Preservation Policies	Archive-PPA
Number of replicas	3.3.5	Replica Check report	Archive-RCA
Backup frequency	3.3.2	Preservation Policies	Archive-PPA
Integrity check frequency	4.2.9	Integrity report	Archive-INTA
Technology evolution	5.1.1.1	Technology Watch Report	Archive-TW
Catalog	4.5.1	Descriptive metadata report	Archive-MA
Transformative migration	4.3.2.1	Designated Community Review	Archive-DCR

Projects that implement ISO 16363 can demonstrate enforcement of NSF style Data Management Plans.

1.3   GENERIC INFRASTRUCTURE FOR MANAGING TECHNOLOGY OBSOLESCENCE

Given a set of policies that enforce trustworthiness, a major remaining challenge is the management of technology evolution. A trustworthy repository must manage the archives independently of the choice of technology (storage systems, databases, authentication systems, access clients, operating systems).

Data grids are software middleware that is installed at each location where data will be managed [15]. Data grids virtualize the properties of a collection, making it possible to control digital object naming, arrangement, access, description, provenance, integrity, retention, replication, and distribution independently of the choice of hardware and software technologies. The ability to interact with multiple types of storage systems, databases, authentication systems, networks, operating systems, and clients make data grids a preferred infrastructure for long-term preservation [11]. Essentially, the properties of an archive can be maintained persistently while technology flows through the archives.

Policy-based data grids use policies and procedures to automate the enforcement of collection properties, the execution of administrative tasks, and the verification of assessment criteria [10]. Policy-based systems are highly extensible, as policies and procedures can be used to control interactions with users, control the properties of an archive, and manage interactions with technology. This capability is essential for enforcing the viewpoint that [9]:

- Preservation is communication with the future.

- Preservation requires the validation of communication from the past.

Policy-based systems explicitly implement management requirements as computer actionable rules, controlled by policies that are applied at Policy Enforcement Points. Every action by a client is trapped at the Policy Enforcement Points, then a rule base is accessed to select the appropriate controlling policy, and an associated computer actionable rule (procedure) is executed. This makes it possible to verify assertions about a repository, such as trustworthiness. Policies can be captured in rule bases, providing an explicit record of the management activities applied to an archive [4, 5, 6, 7, 8]. A future archivist can examine the assertions that were claimed about an archive and verify that the assertions were enforced over time.

The integrated Rule Oriented Data System (iRODS) is a data grid that provides three types of policies that can be used to automate trustworthiness assessment tasks [13, 14, 22,]. They include:

1. Policy Enforcement Point rules. Actions requested by clients are trapped at multiple Policy Enforcement Points. Rules can be defined that are retrieved from a rule base and applied at each Policy Enforcement Point. These rules are named in this document with a ".re" extension.

2. Interactive rules. A rule can be executed interactively, independently of the rules associated with the Policy Enforcement Points. These rules are saved as text files with a ".r" extension, and can be stored in the data grid.

3. Periodic rules. A rule can be queued for either delayed and/or periodic execution. These rules are typically submitted interactively, are also saved as text files with a ".r" extension, and can be stored in the data grid.

A set of rules is defined in this document for the enforcement and validation of trustworthiness assessment criteria. Each ISO 16363 criteria is interpreted as a set of tasks that need to be done. Each task is then mapped to a set of policies that are used to:

- initialize state information required for implementing the criteria;

- apply a procedure to enforce the criteria; and

- validate that the criteria have been successfully enforced.

A descriptive name is used for each rule to define the task that is being automated. Each rule name starts with "rac" to denote repository audit checklist. A description is provided for each rule, along with the persistent state attributes needed to apply the rule and the operations that are executed. Note that rules may be re-used to automate execution of multiple tasks for different ISO criteria. A mapping is provided between the ISO tasks and the rules that are used to identify re-use of rules across tasks. The iRODS (integrated Rule Oriented Data System) rule language is used to implement each rule. Alternate languages that can be used to implement the rules include Javascript, Python, and Haskell.

All policy examples are published as open source software on github, http://github.com, in repository DICE-UNC/policy-workbook/ISO/Rules. Each example is written in the iRODS rule language. Note that the policies may be automatically applied at policy enforcement points, or periodically executed by the iRODS rule engine, or interactively executed by the system administrator.

Chapters 3, 4, and 5 of this document are organized by the major and minor tasks specified by ISO 16363. Chapter 6 provides an example of the implementation of a trustworthy repository, based on the DataNet Federation Consortium federation hub, http://datafed.org.

CHAPTER 2

Trustworthy Repository Description

A repository is described by four sets of information and knowledge.

1. Static properties that define where documents are stored, when documents are audited, and ownership of documents. The static properties are stored as GLOBAL VARIABLES associated with rules.

2. Dynamic properties that define information about each archived record, such as status of processing steps, descriptive metadata, and representation information. Dynamic properties are captured as metadata attributes associated with user names, collection names, and file names.

3. Policies that implement the procedures required to enforce trustworthiness. The policies are written in a rule language and are stored in a rule base.

4. Policy functions that are used to simplify the creation of new rules. The policy functions are listed in the rule file, rac-isoFunctions.re.

2.1   GLOBAL VARIABLES

Global variables are used to specify the properties of the repository. These global variables are used across multiple policies, and need to be defined only once in the rule base. The policies can be configured for use at another repository by modifying the GLOBAL_VARIABLES. Default values are provided to illustrate the use of the GLOBAL_VARIABLES in Table 2.1.

Table 2.1: Global variables defining repository attributes		
Global Variables	**Definition**	**Example**
GLOBAL_ACCOUNT	Home directory for the repository	"/lifelibZone/home/rwmoore"
GLOBAL_ARCHIVES	Sub-collection of *Archive that holds the AIPs	"Archives"
GLOBAL_AUDIT_PERIOD	Period in days for next audit report	"365"
GLOBAL_DIPS	Sub-collection of *Archive that holds the separate metadata files for each AIP	"DIPS"

GLOBAL_EMAIL	E-mail address of person who is notified to conduct a periodic review of the repository management for viability	rwmoore@renci.org
GLOBAL_IMAGES	Sub-collection of GLOBAL_REPOSITORY holding the Docker containers that encapsulate preservation services	"Images"
GLOBAL_MANIFESTS	Sub-collection of GLOBAL_REPOSITORY of *Archive into which manifests are written	"Manifests"
GLOBAL_METADATA	Sub-collection of *Archive that holds the SIP and AIP information files	"Metadata"
GLOBAL_OWNER	Account that has ownership permission on the official reports	"rwmoore"
GLOBAL_REPORTS	Sub-collection of GLOBAL_REPOSITORY or *Archive that holds the repository official reports	"Reports"
GLOBAL_REPOSITORY	Collection holding the repository operations and management documents	"Repository"
GLOBAL_RULES	Sub-collection of GLOBAL-REPOSITORY that holds all of the rules	"Rules"
GLOBAL_SIPS	Sub-collection of *Archive that holds the SIPS	"Sips"
GLOBAL_STORAGE	Storage resource holding repository official reports	"LTLResc"
GLOBAL_VERSIONS	Sub-collection of GLOBAL_REPOSITORY or *Archive that holds prior versions of repository official reports	"Versions"

2.2   METADATA ATTRIBUTES

In addition to the GLOBAL_VARIABLES which represent static information about the repository, metadata attributes are used to define persistent state information required for tracking properties of the archives. The metadata attributes that are specific to the management of trustworthiness are listed in Table 2.2. The attributes are associated with user names (to designate staff properties), collection names (to designate communities), and file names (to designate status of operations). Note that additional persistent state information attributes are used by iRODS to manage the distributed environment.

Table 2.2: Preservation-specific metadata			
Attribute	**Type**	**Meaning**	**Location**
Archive-AIPTemplate	Coll	Name of the template defining the preservation information for a record	Defined on GLOBAL_ACCOUNT/*Archive
Archive-Email	Coll	E-mail address for notifications	Defined on GLOBAL_ACCOUNT/*Archive
Archive-Report	Coll	Time period between updates for archives reports	Defined on GLOBAL_ACCOUNT/*Archive
Archive-Access	Coll	Restrict access to specified person	Defined on GLOBAL_ACCOUNT/*Archive/GLOBAL_ARCHIVES
Archive-CheckHandle	Coll	Process flag set to "1" if a handle is created for an AIP	Defined on GLOBAL_ACCOUNT/*Archive/GLOBAL_ARCHIVES
Archive-Distribution	Coll	Define storage location	Defined on GLOBAL_ACCOUNT/*Archive/GLOBAL_ARCHIVES
Archive-Replication	Coll	Required number of replicas for an AIP	Defined on GLOBAL_ACCOUNT/*Archive/GLOBAL_ARCHIVES
Archive-Description	Coll	Required description for a SIP or AIP	Defined on GLOBAL_ACCOUNT/*Archive/GLOBAL_ARCHIVES & GLOBAL_SIPS
Archive-Format	Coll	Required format for a SIP or AIP. There may be multiple allowed formats.	Defined on GLOBAL_ACCOUNT/*Archive/GLOBAL_ARCHIVES & GLOBAL_SIPS
Archive-IPR	Coll	Account that owns the intellectual property rights for a SIP or AIP	Defined on GLOBAL_ACCOUNT/*Archive/GLOBAL_ARCHIVES & GLOBAL_SIPS
Archive-Ontology	Coll	Ontology name for designated community's collection for a SIP or AIP	Defined on GLOBAL_ACCOUNT/*Archive/GLOBAL_ARCHIVES & GLOBAL_SIPS
Archive-CheckDup	Coll	Flag for whether to check for duplication of a SIP	Defined on GLOBAL_ACCOUNT/*Archive/GLOBAL_SIPS
Archive-CheckFormat	Coll	Flag for whether to verify type of data format	Defined on GLOBAL_ACCOUNT/*Archive/GLOBAL_SIPS

Attribute	Type	Meaning	Location
Archive-CheckIntegrity	Coll	Flag for whether to check integrity	Defined on GLOBAL_ACCOUNT/*Archive/GLOBAL_SIPS
Archive-CheckMetadata	Coll	Flag for whether to verify required metadata	Defined on GLOBAL_ACCOUNT/*Archive/GLOBAL_SIPS
Archive-CheckProtected	Coll	Flag for whether to check for protected data	Defined on GLOBAL_ACCOUNT/*Archive/GLOBAL_SIPS
Archive-Check'virus	Coll	Flag for whether to check for virus	Defined on GLOBAL_ACCOUNT/*Archive/GLOBAL_SIPS
Archive-CheckVocab	Coll	Flag for whether to verify descriptive metadata comply with vocabulary	Defined on GLOBAL_ACCOUNT/*Archive/GLOBAL_SIPS
Audit-Depositor	Coll	Required SIP attribute	Defined on GLOBAL_ACCOUNT/*Archive/GLOBAL_SIPS
Audit-Sources	Coll	Required SIP attribute	Defined on GLOBAL_ACCOUNT/*Archive/GLOBAL_SIPS
Repository-Archives	Coll	Name of a collection for an archive	Defined on GLOBAL_ACCOUNT/ GLOBAL_REPOSITORY
Repository-Email	Coll	E-mail address of repository administrator	Defined on GLOBAL_ACCOUNT/ GLOBAL_REPOSITORY
Repository-Report	Coll	Time period between updates for repository	Defined on GLOBAL_ACCOUNT/ GLOBAL_REPOSITORY
Audit-Distribution	File	Required storage locations for an AIP	Defined on files in GLOBAL_ACCOUNT/*Archive/GLOBAL_ARCHIVES
Audit-Handle	File	Unique ID for a file, using Handle system	Defined on files in GLOBAL_ACCOUNT/*Archive/GLOBAL_ARCHIVES
Audit-Access	File	Read access restricted to specified accounts for an AIP or SIP	Defined on files in GLOBAL_ACCOUNT/*Archive/GLOBAL_ARCHIVES & GLOBAL_SIPS
Audit-CheckDup	File	Status flag set to "1" if a duplicate file is detected when loading a SIP	Defined on files in GLOBAL_ACCOUNT/*Archive/GLOBAL_ARCHIVES & GLOBAL_SIPS

Attribute	Type	Meaning	Location
Audit-CheckFormat	File	Status flag set to "1" if a bad data format is detected in a SIP	Defined on files in GLOBAL_ACCOUNT/*Archive/GLOBAL_ARCHIVES & GLOBAL_SIPS
Audit-CheckIntegrity	File	Status flag set to "1" if an invalid checksum is detected for a SIP	Defined on files in GLOBAL_ACCOUNT/*Archive/GLOBAL_ARCHIVES & GLOBAL_SIPS
Audit-CheckMetadata	File	Status flag set to "1" if missing metadata is detected for a SIP	Defined on files in GLOBAL_ACCOUNT/*Archive/GLOBAL_ARCHIVES & GLOBAL_SIPS
Audit-CheckProtected	File	Status flag set to "1" if protected data is detected in a SIP	Defined on files in GLOBAL_ACCOUNT/*Archive/GLOBAL_ARCHIVES & GLOBAL_SIPS
Audit-CheckVirus	File	Status flag set to "1" if a virus is detected in a SIP	Defined on files in GLOBAL_ACCOUNT/*Archive/GLOBAL_ARCHIVES & GLOBAL_SIPS
Audit-CheckVocab	File	Status flag set to "1" when metadata do not comply with HIVE when loading a SIP	Defined on files in GLOBAL_ACCOUNT/*Archive/GLOBAL_ARCHIVES & GLOBAL_SIPS
Audit-Comply	File	Flag for a SIP or AIP denoting processing steps were passed	Defined on files in GLOBAL_ACCOUNT/*Archive/GLOBAL_ARCHIVES & GLOBAL_SIPS
Audit-Depositor	File	Depositor of a SIP or AIP	Defined on files in GLOBAL_ACCOUNT/*Archive/GLOBAL_ARCHIVES & GLOBAL_SIPS
Audit-Description	File	Description of a SIP or AIP	Defined on files in GLOBAL_ACCOUNT/*Archive/GLOBAL_ARCHIVES & GLOBAL_SIPS
Audit-Ontology	File	Ontology name for designated community's collection for a SIP or AIP	Defined on files in GLOBAL_ACCOUNT/*Archive/GLOBAL_ARCHIVES & GLOBAL_SIPS
Audit-Source	File	Source of a SIP or AIP	Defined on files in GLOBAL_ACCOUNT/*Archive/GLOBAL_ARCHIVES & GLOBAL_SIPS

Attribute	Type	Meaning	Location
Audit-Date	File	Date stamp for when a report should be updated	Defined on files in GLOBAL_REPORTS & GLOBAL_MAN-IFESTS
Repository-Course	User	List of courses taken by repository staff member	Defined on staff members
Repository-Devel-Date	User	Date stamp for when the next development course should be done, in Unix format	Defined on staff members
Repository-Role	User	Allowed roles: "Archive-manager", "Archive-archivist", "Archive-admin", "Archive-IT"	Defined on staff members

An example of a preservation attribute is the collection name that is used for each archive. Since there may be multiple archives associated with a repository, the names of the archives are found by a query on the GLOBAL_REPOSITORY collection for the values of the metadata attribute Repository-Archives. New archives can be added dynamically to the repository, with each new repository name entered as metadata on the GLOBAL_REPOSITORY collection. (See Policy35, rac-setArchives.r.)

2.3   DOCUMENTS

A principal component of ISO 16363 is the definition of a set of 80 documents that are required for validating trustworthiness. There are two types of reports specified in the standard: management documents (47 in total) that specify how the repository will be managed, and assessment reports (33 in total) that can be automatically generated. A list of the required reports is shown in Table 2.3, along with the corresponding section in the ISO standard for which the report is generated. A unique name that begins with the characters "Archive-" is specified for each report. Also in Table 2.3, the Source column designates whether the document is a management report that is created outside of the repository, but managed within the repository (External), or whether the document is automatically generated within the repository by procedures running as computer actionable rules (Version or Manifest). Manifest reports are logs of all operations of a given type. Version reports summarize properties at a given time, with each summarization stored as a separate report. The column labeled "A" denotes those reports that are specific to an archives.

Table 2.3: ISO 16363 Reports				
ISO	**Report Name**	**Report Contents**	**Source**	**Archive**
3.1	Archive-SSA	Status of all documents	Version	
3.1.1	Archive-MS	Mission Statement	External	
3.1.2	Archive-PSP	Preservation Strategic Plan	External	
3.1.2.1	Archive-CP	Contingency Plan	External	
3.1.2.1	Archive-EAP	Escrow Arrangement Plan	External	
3.1.2.1	Archive-SP	Succession Plan	External	
3.1.2.2	Archive-NPRA	Notifications of Periodic Review	Manifest	
3.1.3	Archive-CollP	Collection Policy	External	
3.2.1	Archive-OP	Operations Plan	External	
3.2.1.1	Archive-STFP	Staffing Plan	External	
3.2.1.3	Archive-SE	Staff Experience report	External	
3.2.1.3	Archive-SEA	Staff Experience audit	Manifest	
3.3.1	Archive-DCP	Designated Community	External	A
3.3.2	Archive-RAA	Repository Action report	Manifest	
3.3.2	Archive-PMA	Micro-services report	Version	
3.3.2	Archive-PPRS	Registered policies	Version	
3.3.2.1	Archive-PIP	Preservation Implementation Plan (versions)	External	
3.3.2.1	Archive-TC	Technology/Community report – surveys	External	
3.3.2.1	Archive-PPA	Preservation Policies (rule base)	Version	
3.3.3	Archive-IA	Infrastructure Acquisition report	External	
3.3.3	Archive-IRA	Infrastructure Used report	Version	A
3.3.4	Archive-TAR	Technical audit reports	External	
3.3.5	Archive-RCA	Replica Check report	Manifest	
3.3.6	Archive-CR	Certification reports	External	
3.4.1	Archive-BPR	Business Planning report	External	
3.4.2	Archive-BR	Budget report	External	
3.4.2	Archive-FAR	Financial Audit report	External	
3.4.3	Archive-FR	Financial Risk report	External	
3.5.1	Archive-SL	Service Level Agreement report	External	A
3.5.1.1	Archive-DAR	Deposit Agreement report (metadata)	External	A
3.5.1.2	Archive-SAR	Submission Agreement report	External	A
3.5.1.2	Archive-SOP	Standard Operating Procedure	External	
3.5.1.3	Archive-CFR	Confirmation report	External	A

ISO	Report Name	Report Contents	Source	Archive
3.5.1.4	Archive-DD	Disputed Data set report	External	A
3.5.1.4	Archive-ALRA	Access list	Manifest	A
3.5.1.4	Archive-DIDA	Disputed Data set audit	Version	A
3.5.2	Archive-IP	Intellectual Property report	External	A
3.5.2	Archive-IPA	Intellectual Property Audit	Manifest	A
4.1.1	Archive-INP	Information Properties report	External	A
4.1.1	Archive-PMRA	Policy Metadata Report	Version	A
4.1.1.1	Archive-AU	Authenticity requirements report	External	A
4.1.1.2	Archive-CIRA	Content Information Deposition report	Version	A
4.1.2	Archive-CID	Content Information report	External	A
4.1.3	Archive-SIP	SIP template for required metadata	External	A
4.1.3	Archive-SSR	SIP Submission Requirements report	External	A
4.1.4	Archive-CINCA	Content Information Non-Compliance report	Version	A
4.1.5	Archive-META	Metadata records for SIPs and AIPs	External	A
4.1.5	Archive-SIP-CRA	SIP compliance report	Manifest	A
4.1.6	Archive-ARA	Archives Content report	Version	A
4.1.7	Archive-SIA	SIP Ingestion Audit report	Manifest	A
4.1.8	Archive-PAA	Preservation Action Audit report	Manifest	A
4.2.1	Archive-AIP	AIP template for required metadata	External	A
4.2.2	Archive-STAR	SIP to AIP Process Description report	External	A
4.2.3.1	Archive-SAPA	SIP Disposition Audit report	Version	A
4.2.4.1	Archive-IDCA	Handle Duplicate Audit report	Version	A
4.2.7.1	Archive-HVOA	HIVE Vocabulary Ontology	Version	A
4.2.8	Archive-AIP-CRA	AIP Compliance report	Manifest	A
4.2.9	Archive-INTA	Integrity Report	Manifest	A
4.2.10	Archive-ARUA	Audit Report of all actions	Version	A
4.3.2.1	Archive-DCR	Designated Community Review	External	A
4.4.1	Archive-BDA	Format conversion support report	Manifest	A
4.4.1	Archive-DIRA	Docker Image report	Manifest	
4.5.1	Archive-MA	Descriptive metadata report	Version	A
4.6.1	Archive-ALA	Access log	Version	A

ISO	Report Name	Report Contents	Source	Archive
4.6.1.1	Archive-AFA	Access Failure report	Version	A
4.6.2	Archive-DIP	DIP template for required metadata	External	A
4.6.2.1	Archive-ERR	Error reports	External	
5.1.1	Archive-IRL	Technology Risk report	External	
5.1.1	Archive-ILA	Infrastructure List report	Version	
5.1.1.1	Archive-TW	Technology Watch report	External	
5.1.1.1.2	Archive-URA	Usage report	Version	A
5.1.1.1.3	Archive-PL	Technology Change report	External	
5.1.1.1.4	Archive-TSE	Test System Evaluation report	External	
5.1.1.1.6	Archive-APU	Audit of Performance	External	
5.1.1.4	Archive-PR	Security Patch report	External	
5.1.1.6	Archive-TRA	Traceability report (operations/state)	Version	A
5.1.1.6.1	Archive-CM	Change Management report	External	
5.1.1.6.2	Archive-QAR	Process Verification report	External	
5.2.1	Archive-SRF	Security Risk Factors	External	
5.2.2	Archive-CE	ISO 17799 certification	External	

Given the values of Source and Archive the storage locations for the reports are given by:

Source	Archive	Location
External		GLOBAL_ACCOUNT/GLOBAL_REPOSITORY/GLOBAL_REPORTS
External	A	GLOBAL_ACCOUNT/*Archive/GLOBAL_REPORTS
Version		GLOBAL_ACCOUNT/GLOBAL_REPOSITORY/GLOBAL_REPORTS
Version	A	GLOBAL_ACCOUNT/*Archive/GLOBAL_REPORTS
Manifest		GLOBAL_ACCOUNT/GLOBAL_REPOSITORY/GLOBAL_MANIFESTS
Manifest	A	GLOBAL_ACCOUNT/*Archive/GLOBAL_MANIFESTS

Note there are two externally generated reports that are manifests, Archive-ERR and Archive-PL, that are stored in

GLOBAL_ACCOUNT/GLOBAL_REPOSITORY/GLOBAL_MANIFESTS.

For each report of the type "External", the information items that should be included in the report are defined. Each information item is annotated with a label to denote its use:

- Repository – item is used to define repository administrative requirements

- Operations – item is used to define operations requirements

• Archives – item is used to define requirements for the archived objects

The documents are stored in a standard location within the archives given by the collection hierarchy:

GLOBAL_ACCOUNT

    GLOBAL_REPOSITORY

        GLOBAL_REPORTS

        GLOBAL_VERSIONS

        GLOBAL_MANIFESTS

        GLOBAL_RULES

        GLOBAL_IMAGES

   *Archive

        GLOBAL_REPORTS

        GLOBAL_VERSIONS

        GLOBAL_MANIFESTS

        GLOBAL_METADATA

        GLOBAL_SIPS

        GLOBAL_ARCHIVES

        GLOBAL_DIPS

where the *Archive name is registered in the Repository-Archives metadata attribute on the GLOBAL_REPOSITORY collection. Each project archive is stored in a separate collection. Each sub-collection holds a specific type of digital object:

GLOBAL_REPORTS	Holds all documents that will be versioned
GLOBAL_VERSIONS	Holds the versions of the documents
GLOBAL_MANIFESTS	Holds the manifests/log files
GLOBAL_RULES	Holds copies of the rules used by the repository
GLOBAL_IMAGES	Holds virtual machine images of the preservation services
GLOBAL_METADATA	Holds the metadata files that provide descriptive, representation, and provenance information
GLOBAL_SIPS	Holds the Submission Information Packages
GLOBAL_AIPS	Holds the Archival Information Packages
GLOBAL_DIPS	Holds the Dissemination Information Packages

Note this collection structure allows the creation of AIPs that are different from SIPS. Also, the documents pertaining to the operation of a specific archived collection are organized together under the associated archive name, *Archive. Documents related to the operations of the repository are stored under the collection GLOBAL_REPOSITORY.

2.4   POLICIES

There is a set of policies that is needed to enable the management of all of the required documents. These policies automate a generic set of eleven tasks related to document storage, versioning, access, and notification. They include:

- Policy1 – rac-storeReportVersion.re (replaced by Policy26)

  ○ Store a versioned copy of a document (enforced on document submission) in GLOBAL_REPOSITORY/GLOBAL_VERSIONS or *Archive/GLOBAL_ VERSIONS.

- Policy2 – rac-setReportUpdateDate.re (replaced by Policy26)

  ○ Set the date when a new versioned copy is required (enforced on document submission). This rule includes the Policy1 operations for versioning documents.

- Policy3 – rac-verifyReportUpdates.r

  ○ Verify that updates have been done for a specific document.

- Policy4 – rac-accessReportVersion.r

  ○ Access the most recent version of a document and list all versions.

- Policy5 – rac-checkReportExists.r

  ○ Check that a given document exists and identify the update date.

- Policy6 – rac-generateReportNotifications.r

  ○ Maintain a manifest, Archive-NPRA, of e-mail notifications for management review. Send notifications each year for updates to a specified plan. The report is stored in GLOBAL_ACCOUNT/GLOBAL_REPOSITORY/GLOBAL_MANIFESTS.

- Policy7 – rac-generateReportStatus.r

  ○ Generate a status report for all of the required documents, saved as Arhive-SSA in the collection GLOBAL_ACCOUNT/GLOBAL_REPOSITORY/GLOBAL_REPORTS.

- Policy8 – rac-setReportAuditPeriod.r

  ○ Set the Repository-Report period as an attribute on the collection GLOBAL_ REPOSITORY or set Archive-Report as an attribute on *Archive to define the time interval between audits.

- Policy26 – rac-setChecksum.re

  ○ Set the date when a new versioned copy is required, version the document, and set a checksum each time a document is submitted to a GLOBAL_REPORTS collection. This replaces Policy1 and Policy2.

- Policy35 – rac-setArchives.r

  ○ Add the name of an archives to the collection GLOBAL_REPOSITORY using the metadata attribute Repository-Archives and create the new archives collection.

- Policy36 – rac-setAuditDate.r

  ○ Set the Audit-Date on a document.

- Policy80 – rac-setAuditDateColl.r

  ○ Set the Audit-Date on all files in a collection.

- Policy55 – rac-saveManifests.r

  ○ Version all manifests, and start new manifest files. The rule is used to manage archiving of large manifest files.

2.5   POLICY FUNCTIONS

In order to simplify the creation of rules, policy functions have been developed to execute repetitive tasks. The policy functions are listed below. Preservation policy functions use the GLOBAL variables to manage the storage of the required documents. The twenty-three preservation policy functions are:

racCheckArchive (*Archive, *Stat) – check whether a valid *Archive name is specified. The name must be in the list of Repository-Archives metadata values on the collection GLOBAL_ACCOUNT/GLOBAL_REPOSITORY.

racCheckMsg (*Msg, *Msgt) – remove minus signs and under-bars from e-mail messages. The input message, *Msg is transformed into *Msgt.

racCheckNumReplicas (*Res, *Num) – return the number of replicas created by the resource *Res in *Num.

racCreateHandle (*Coll, *File) – create a unique ID for a file, *File, in collection, *Coll using the Handle system. The ID is registered on the file as the metadata attribute Audit-Handle.

racDupCheck (*File, *Coll, *Archive, *S8) – check whether a SIP specified by "*Coll/*File" is a duplicate of an existing AIP in the archive, *Archive. The return value, *S8, is set to "1" if a duplicate exists, and is set to "2" if there is no duplicate.

racFindRep (*Coll, *Rep) – identify the repository that is referenced by the collection, *Coll. The name is returned in *Rep and may either be GLOBAL_REPOSITORY or an archive name, *Archive. The function:

- compares the collection name to GLOBAL_ACCOUNT/GLOBAL_REPOSITORY/GLOBAL_REPORTS and to GLOBAL_ACCOUNT/*Archive/GLOBAL_REPORTS where the values for *Archive are retrieved from the Repository-Archives attribute on the GLOBAL_REPOSITORY collection; and

- returns either GLOBAL_REPOSITORY or the name of *Archive in the variable *Rep.

racFindRepColl (*File, *Rep) – identify the collection that houses a document based on a list of manifests. The head of *File (characters before the extension) is compared to the list of manifests. If a match is found, *Rep is set to "GLOBAL_MANIFESTS, otherwise *Rep is set to GLOBAL_REPORTS. The function:

- extracts the head of the file using the policy function SplitPathByKey; and

- compares with the lists:

  ○ # list of generated reports that are not archive specific and are manifests

    "DIRA", "ERR", "NPRA", "PL", "RAA", "RCA", "SEA"; and

  ○ # list of generated reports that are archive specific and are manifests

    "AIPCRA", "ALRA", "BDA", "INTA", "IPA", "PAA", "SIA", "SIPCRA".

racFormatCheck (*File, *Coll, *Archive, S4) – check whether a SIP specified by "*Coll/*File" has a required data format, specified by the attribute Archive-Format on the GLOBAL_SIPS collection. The return value *S4 is set to "1" for an error, and to "2" if the format complies with the required value.

racGetAVUMetadata (*Archive, *Coll, *Name, *Cont, *Val) – retrieve the metadata *Name from *Coll for archive *Archive and return the value in *Val. Send notification of a missing attribute if *Cont = "1".

racGlobalSet () – Defines the global variables.

racIntegrityCheck (*File, *Coll, *Archive, *S7) – check a SIP specified by "*Coll/*File" for integrity. The return value, *S7, is set to "1" if the file is corrupted, and to "2" if the checksum is good.

racMetadataCheck (*File, *Coll, *Archive, *S5) – check whether a SIP specified by "*Coll/*File" has all required metadata. The return value, *S5, is set to "1" if metadata are missing, and to "2" if required metadata are present.

racNotify (*Archive, *Msg) – send e-mail notification to the repository administrator for the archive, *Archive. Stdout is copied to the body of the E-mail. The header message, *Msg, is modified to remove minus signs and colons using the racCheckMessage policy function. The rac-Notify function retrieves the address from GLOBAL_ACCOUNT/*Archive from the attribute Archive-Email. If the address is not set, an error message is sent to the Repository Administrator, using the address Repository-Email set on the GLOBAL_ACCOUNT/GLOBAL_REPOSITORY collection. All notifications are logged in Archive-PAA and stored under GLOBAL_ACCOUNT/*Archive/GLOBAL_MANIFESTS.

racProtectedDataCheck (*File, *Coll, *Archive, *S3) – check a SIP specified by "*Coll/*-File" in archive, *Archive, for presence of protected data such as PII, PCI, or PHI. The analysis is done at the storage location where the SIP is stored. The return value, *S3, is set to "1" if protected data are present, and to "2" if there are no protected data.

racReservedVocabCheck (*File, *Coll, *Archive, *S6) – check whether a SIP specified by "*Coll/*File" in archive, *Archive, uses an approved vocabulary for descriptive metadata terms. The return value, *S6, is set to "1" if unknown terms are used and to "2" if the terms comply with a reserved vocabulary.

racSaveFile (*File, *Rep) – save the contents of stdout to *File in the GLOBAL_ACCOUNT/*Rep/GLOBAL_REPORTS collection and create a version of the file in the GLOBAL_ACCOUNT/*Rep/GLOBAL_VERSIONS collection. This function is called every time a report is generated. The function:

- checks which collection should hold the report, GLOBAL_REPOSITORY or *Archive;

- creates GLOBAL_REPORTS directory if needed;

- creates GLOBAL_VERSIONS directory if needed;

- copies stdout to *File;

- stores *File in GLOBAL_REPORTS;

- checksums the file *File;

- replicates the file *File;

- versions the file *File, storing a version in the GLOBAL_VERSIONS collection;

- sets a default Repository-Report attribute on the collection GLOBAL_REPOS-ITORY or the Archive-Report attribute on *Archive if no default audit period is specified;

- sets an Audit-Date attribute for when a report should be updated;

- verifies the checksum of the versioned file;

- replicates the versioned file; and

- verifies the checksum of the replica of the versioned file

racSetAuditDateFile (*File, *Colh, *Coll, *Tim) – set the Audit-Date attribute on "*Coll/*-File" using the current time given by *Tim. The function:

- retrieves a time period from the attribute Archive-Report or Repository-Report from collection *Colh;

- creates a new audit time by adding the time period to the current time, *Tim;

- removes all existing Audit-Date attributes from the file in *Coll/*File; and

- sets the new Audit-Date attribute on the file.

racSplitArchive (*Coll, *Archive) – find the archive referenced by a collection name. The name of the *Archive is found by deleting GLOBAL_ACCOUNT/ from the head of the collection. The name is validated by comparing with the values of the attribute Repository-Archives on the GLOBAL_ACCOUNT/GLOBAL_REPOSITORY collection.

racVerifyAuditReport (*Coll, *Tim) – check that the attribute Repository-Report or Archive-Report is defined on collection *Coll. The function:

- creates an audit period from GLOBAL_AUDIT_PERIOD, the number of days in the future for the audit;

- checks whether the attribute Repository-Report or Archive-Report is defined for collection *Coll; and

- if a value is missing, a new audit period is created for the attribute Repository-Report or Archive-Report.

racVersionFile (*File, *Rep, *Coll) – create a version of *Coll/*File in GLOBAL_AC-COUNT/*Rep/GLOBAL_VERSIONS. This function encapsulates the algorithm for creating the version name, creates the version, and sets the access control. The function:

- uses the file in *Coll/*File;

- creates the destination collection name from GLOBAL_ACCOUNT/*Rep/ GLOBAL_VERSIONS;

- creates the destination collection if necessary;

- searches for prior versions of the file;

- finds the most recent version number;

- increments the version number and creates the destination path name;

- copies *File into the destination path; and

- sets the ownership to GLOBAL_OWNER.

racVirusCheck (*File, *Coll, *S2) – check a SIP specified by "*Coll/*File" for presence of a virus. The function is applied at the remote storage location where the SIP is stored. The return value, *S2, is set to "1" if a virus is present, and to "2" if no virus is detected.

racWriteManifest (*OutFile, *Rep, *Source) – append the contents of *Source to the file *OutFile in the collection GLOBAL_ACCOUNT/*Rep/GLOBAL_MANIFESTS. This function is called every time a manifest file is updated. The function:

- creates the storage collection name as GLOBAL_ACCOUNT/*Rep/GLOBAL_MANIFESTS;

- creates GLOBAL_MANIFESTS directory if needed;

- creates the manifest file, *OutFile, if needed, in the collection GLOBAL_MANIFESTS;

- appends the information in *Source to the end of *OutFile;

- resets the checksum of the manifest file;

- updates the replica of the manifest file; and

- verifies the checksum of the replica of the versioned file.

splitPathByKey (*Name, *Delim, *Head, *Tail) – split a string at the delimiter, *Delim, into a head, *Head, and a tail, *Tail. Note that the msiSplitPathByKey micro-service requires that the delimiter be present in the name and throws an error if the delimiter is not present. The function:

- parses the string checking for the delimiter, starting from the end of the string; and

- returns the head and tail. Note that either the head or the tail may be null.

CHAPTER 3

ISO 16363 Organizational Infrastructure

Section 3 of the ISO 16363 standard examines requirements for Organizational Infrastructure management. Most of the requirements require the creation of an external document that can be managed within the repository.

3.1 GOVERNANCE AND ORGANIZATIONAL VIABILITY

The documents that provide information to funders, depositors, and users about the governance and organizational viability are described in Section 3.1. These include:

Status of all documents	Archive-SSA	ISO 3.1
Mission Statement	Archive-MS	ISO 3.1.1
Preservation Strategic Plan	Archive-PSP	ISO 3.1.2
Contingency Plan	Archive-CP	ISO 3.1.2.1
Escrow Arrangement Plan	Archive-EAP	ISO 3.1.2.1
Succession Plan	Archive-SP	ISO 3.1.2.1
Notifications of Periodic Review	Archive-NPRA	ISO 3.1.2.2
Collection Policy	Archive-CollP	ISO 3.1.3

3.1.1 THE REPOSITORY SHALL HAVE A MISSION STATEMENT THAT REFLECTS A COMMITMENT TO THE PRESERVATION OF, LONG-TERM RETENTION OF, MANAGEMENT OF, AND ACCESS TO DIGITAL INFORMATION

Report creation: The Mission Statement (Archive-MS) is a management report that is generated externally by the management team. The document contains:

Repository – Documentation of mission statement
Repository – Documentation of regulatory mandates for preservation
Repository – Documentation of repository charter
Repository – Formal commitment to long-term preservation
Repository – Formal commitment to retention, management, and access

The report is stored in
GLOBAL_ACCOUNT/GLOBAL_REPOSITORY/GLOBAL_REPORTS.

Property Management: The report is managed by:

- Policy4 – rac-accessReportVersion.r

   ◦ Access the most recent version of a document for an archive and list all versions. The action is logged in Archive-PAA.

- Policy5 – rac-checkReportExists.r

   ◦ Check that a given document exists for an archive and identify the update date. The action is logged in Archive-PAA.

- Policy6 – rac-generateReportNotifications.r

   ◦ Maintain a manifest, Archive-NPRA, of e-mail notifications for management review. Send notifications each year for updates to a specified plan.

- Policy7 – rac-generateReportStatus.r

   ◦ Generate a status report for all of the required documents, saved as Archive-SSA in the GLOBAL_REPOSITORY/GLOBAL_REPORTS folder.

- Policy8 – rac-setReportAuditPeriod.r

   ◦ Set the Repository-Report period as an attribute on the collection GLOBAL_REPOSITORY or Archive-Report as an attribute on the collection *Archive. The action is logged in Archive-RAA.

- Policy26 – rac-setChecksum.re

   ◦ Set the date when a new versioned copy is required, version the document, and set a checksum each time a document is submitted to a GLOBAL_REPORTS collection. This replaces Policy1 and Policy2.

- Policy35 – rac-setArchives.r

   ◦ Add the name of an archives to the collection GLOBAL_REPOSITORY using the metadata attribute Repository-Archives and create the new archives collection. The action is logged in Archive-RAA.

- Policy36 – rac-setAuditDate.r

- ° Set the Audit-Date on a document. The action is logged in either Archive-PAA or Archive-RAA depending on the collection.

- Policy55 – rac-saveManifests.r

  - ° Version all manifests, and start new manifest files.

Property Assessment: The report is assessed by:

- Policy3 – rac-verifyReportUpdates.r

  - ° Verify that updates have been done for a specific document. The action is logged in Archive-PAA.

- Policy6 – rac-generateReportNotifications.r

  - ° Maintain a manifest, Archive-NPRA, of e-mail notifications for management review. Send notifications each year for updates to a specified plan.

3.1.2 THE REPOSITORY SHALL HAVE A PRESERVATION STRATEGIC PLAN THAT DEFINES THE APPROACH THE REPOSITORY WILL TAKE IN THE LONG-TERM SUPPORT OF ITS MISSION

Report creation: The Preservation Strategic Plan (Archive-PSP) is a management report that is generated externally by the management team. The document contains:

Operations – History of administrative decisions
Operations – History of preservation planning – meeting minutes
Repository – Documentation of approach for long-term preservation
Repository – Documentation of the approach for resource allocation

The report is managed and assessed by Policy3-Policy8, Policy26, Policy35, and Policy36 and stored in
GLOBAL_ACCOUNT/GLOBAL_REPOSITORY/GLOBAL_REPORTS.

3.1.2.1 The repository shall have an appropriate, formal succession plan, contingency plans, and/ or escrow arrangements in place in case the repository ceases to operate or the governing or funding institution substantially changes its scope.

Report creation: Three management documents are required: Succession Plan (Archive-SP), Contingency Plan (Archive-CP), and Escrow Arrangement Plan (Archive-EAP). The three documents are generated externally by the management team.

The Succession Plan (Archive-SP) contains:

Archives – Policies for ensuring complete transfer of the management responsibility
Repository – Formal agreements with successor organizations for transfer of the repository

The Contingency Plan (Archive-CP) contains:

Archives – Procedures for granting requisite rights
Operations – History of the contingency plan evolution
Repository – Documentation of purpose for the repository
Repository – Documentation of steps that will be taken to ensure continuity of the repository
Repository – Documentation of the intent to ensure continuity of the repository

The Escrow Arrangement Plan (Archive-EAP) contains:

Operations – Documentation of components needed to enable reconstitution of the repository
Repository – Escrow arrangement for funding that is set aside for contingencies
Repository – Escrow arrangements for critical code
Repository – Escrow arrangements for metadata

The documents are managed by Policy3-Policy8, Policy26, Policy35, and Policy36 and are stored in GLOBAL_ACCOUNT/GLOBAL_REPOSITORY/GLOBAL_REPORTS.

3.1.2.2 *The repository shall monitor its organizational environment to determine when to execute its formal succession plan, contingency plans, and/or escrow arrangements.*

In addition to an update period required for reviewing each of the succession, contingency, and escrow arrangement plans, a review is also needed of the state of the organization. The organization review should be done periodically to verify that the repository management is still viable.

Instead of implementing an update period as an attribute on the GLOBAL_REPOSITORY collection, we can use a rule that sends a notification e-mail message periodically to the system administrator to schedule an organization review. The rule Policy6, rac-generateReportNotifications, sets up a periodic notification every year. The rule is run once, and is then automatically executed yearly by the rule engine.

The rule uses a GLOBAL_EMAIL variable to identify the e-mail address of the system administrator. Each time the rule executes, a manifest file that tracks notifications is updated. The manifest file is stored at GLOBAL_ACCOUNT/GLOBAL_REPOSITORY/GLOBAL_MANIFESTS/Archive-NPRA.

Property Management:

- Policy6 – rac-generateReportNotifications.r

  ○ Maintain a manifest, Archive-NPRA, of e-mail notifications for management review. Send notifications each year for updates to a specified plan.

3.1.3 THE REPOSITORY SHALL HAVE A COLLECTION POLICY OR OTHER DOCUMENT THAT SPECIFIES THE TYPE OF INFORMATION IT WILL PRESERVE, RETAIN, MANAGE, AND PROVIDE ACCESS TO

Report creation: The Collection Policy Plan (Archive-CollP) is a management report that is generated externally by the management team. The document should identify the type of digital objects that will be managed by the repository, the required provenance, descriptive, and representation information, and the required parsing and display applications. The document contains:

Repository – Documentation of vision for the repository
Repository – Documentation of goals for the repository
Repository – Documentation of guidance on acquisition of digital content
Repository – Documentation of the type of information that will be preserved

The Collection Policy Plan (Archive-CollP) is managed by Policy3-Policy8, Policy26, Policy35, and Policy36 and is stored in GLOBAL_ACCOUNT/GLOBAL_REPOSITORY/GLOBAL_REPORTS.

3.2 ORGANIZATIONAL STRUCTURE AND STAFFING

The documents that provide information about Organizational Structure and Staffing are described in Section 3.2.

Operations Plan	Archive-OP	ISO 3.2.1
Staffing Plan	Archive-STFP	ISO 3.2.1.1
Staff Experience report	Archive-SE	ISO 3.2.1.3
Staff Experience audit	Archive-SEA	ISO 3.2.1.3

3.2.1 THE REPOSITORY SHALL HAVE IDENTIFIED AND ESTABLISHED THE DUTIES THAT IT NEEDS TO PERFORM AND SHALL HAVE APPOINTED STAFF WITH ADEQUATE SKILLS AND EXPERIENCE TO FULFILL THESE DUTIES

Report creation: The Operations Plan (Archive-OP) is a management report that is generated externally by the management team. The duties that need to be performed by the repository staff are typically specified by a Concept of Operations plan, and include definitions of the staff that will be responsible for each duty. The report should be revised periodically to track changes in the requirements for the repository. The Operations Plan contains definitions of roles and responsibilities, and plans for repository development. Required levels of training and accreditation are defined for staff members. The types of information include:

Operations – Analysis comparing staffing levels to industry standards
Operations – Concept of operations
Operations – Documentation of duties that need to be performed
Operations – Documentation of organizational charts
Operations – Documentation of roles and responsibilities
Operations – Staff expertise development plans
Repository – Plans for the repository development

The document is managed by Policy3-Policy8, Policy26, Policy35, and Policy36 and is stored in GLOBAL_ACCOUNT/GLOBAL_REPOSITORY/GLOBAL_REPORTS.

3.2.1.1 *The repository shall have identified and established the duties that it needs to perform.*

Repository duties are listed in the archive operations plan, Archive-OP. The staff that performs the duties can be classified as:

- defining preservation policies, done by the Manager;

- managing accession of collections and formation of AIPs, done by an Archivist. The number of Archivists that are needed is related to the number and status of collections;

- managing repository, done by Admin; and

- managing infrastructure for security, compute, storage, and networking, done by IT staff.

A staffing plan can be implemented independently of the Concept of Operations. The plan is called Archive-STFP and includes:

| Operations – Certificates required for training and accreditation |
| Operations – Documentation of job descriptions |
| Operations – History of review audits |
| Operations – Staff professional development plans |

The staffing plan (Archive-STFP) is managed using Policy3-Policy8, Policy26, Policy35, and Policy36, and is stored in GLOBAL_ACCOUNT/GLOBAL_REPOSITORY/GLOBAL_REPORTS.

3.2.1.2 *The repository shall have the appropriate number of staff to support all functions and services.*

To track the number of staff required for each duty, a method is needed to assign roles to persons, count the number of persons in each role, and list the persons that have a given role.

Property Creation:

- Policy9 – rac-setRole.r

  ○ Set an attribute on a user name that specifies their role, "Repository-Role." Allowed values are "Archive-manager", "Archive-archivist", "Archive-admin", "Archive-IT". The action is logged in Archive-RAA.

Property Assessment:

- Policy10 – rac-listRoles.r

  ○ Count the number of persons in each role and list their names and access roles. The report is saved in Archive-SEA, Staff Experience Audit in GLOBAL_ACCOUNT/GLOBAL_REPOSITORY/GLOBAL_MANIFESTS.

3.2.1.3 *The repository shall have in place an active professional development program that provides staff with skills and expertise development opportunities.*

Tracking the professional development of each staff member can be done by assigning a yearly requirement to take a development course. A Staff Experience Report (Archive-SE) defines the plans for professional development, and tracks the staff training budget and expenditures. The Staff Experience Report includes:

| Operations – Certificates awarded for training and accreditation |
| Operations – Documentation of performance goals |
| Operations – Plans for professional development and reports |

| Operations – Staff achievements |
| Operations – Staff assignments |
| Operations – Staff training expenditure |
| Operations – Staff training requirements and training budgets |

The Staff Experience Report (Archive-SE) is managed by Policy3-Policy8, Policy26, Policy35, and Policy36 and is stored in GLOBAL_ACCOUNT/GLOBAL_REPOSITORY/GLOBAL_REPORTS.

A second document is needed to audit the number of staff working on the archive. The Staff Experience Audit (Archive-SEA) maintains a list of all development activities completed each year. The audit report is generated by Policy12, rac-listDevelopment.r.

Property Creation:

- Policy11 – rac-setDevelopmentDate.r

  ○ Set an attribute on a repository staff name, "Repository-Devel-Date", that specifies the date for completion of a development course. The action is logged in Archive-SEA.

- Policy12 – rac-listDevelopment.r

  ○ List the development courses and their completion dates for each repository staff member in a Staff Experience Audit report, Archive-SEA, stored in GLOBAL_ACCOUNT/GLOBAL_REPOSITORY/GLOBAL_MANIFESTS.

Property Management:

- Policy13 – rac-recordDevelopment.r

  ○ Add an attribute to a repository staff name for each completed course, "Repository-Course", along with the date. The action is logged in Archive-SEA.

3.3   PROCEDURAL ACCOUNTABILITY AND PRESERVATION

The documents that describe procedural accountability and preservation are described in Section 3.3.

Designated Community	Archive-DCP	ISO 3.3.1
Preservation Policies (rule base)	Archive-PPA	ISO 3.3.2
Repository Action report	Archive-RAA	ISO 3.3.2
Micro-services report	Archive-PMA	ISO 3.3.2
Registered policies	Archive-PPRS	ISO 3.3.2

Preservation Implementation Plan (versions)	Archive-PIP	ISO 3.3.2.1
Technology/Community report – surveys	Archive-TC	ISO 3.3.2.1
Technical audit reports	Archive-TAR	ISO 3.3.4
Replica Check report	Archive-RCA	ISO 3.3.5
Certification reports	Archive-CR	ISO 3.3.6

3.3.1   THE REPOSITORY SHALL HAVE DEFINED ITS DESIGNATED COMMUNITY AND ASSOCIATED KNOWLEDGE BASE(S) AND SHALL HAVE THSE DEFINITIONS APPROPRIATELY ACCESSIBLE

The knowledge base associated with a designated community can be represented as an ontology that is registered into the Helping Interdisciplinary Vocabulary Engineering system (HIVE). Each descriptive term used for an AIP can be compared with the HIVE ontology to verify compliance with the terms used by the designated community. The designated community is represented by the corresponding ontology name, stored as the attribute, Archive-Ontology, on the collection that holds the community's archives. A Designated Community report, called Archive-DCP, documents the designated communities that access the archives, their knowledge repositories, and their archives. The Designated Community report (Archive-DCP) contains:

Archives – Documentation of the associated knowledge bases
Archives – Documentation of the Designated Community

The Designated Community report is managed by Policy3-Policy8, Policy26, Policy35, and Policy36. The report is stored in GLOBAL_ACCOUNT/*Archive/GLOBAL_REPORTS.

Property Creation:

- Policy14 – rac-setCommunityOntology.r

  ◦ The ontology required by a Designated Community is registered as an attribute, Archive-Ontology, on the *Archive collection. The action is logged in Archive-PAA.

Property Assessment:

- Policy15 – rac-listOntologies.r

  ◦ The ontologies used by all Designated Communities are listed along with the collection name. The action is logged in Archive-RAA.

3.3.2   THE REPOSITORY SHALL HAVE PRESERVATION POLICIES IN PLACE TO ENSURE ITS PRESERVATION STRATEGIC PLAN WILL BE MET

The Mission Statement, Archive-MS, defines the preservation mission. A policy-based data management system automates the duties that the repository needs to perform by developing policies to execute each task. The set of policies then serves as a proxy for the preservation strategic plan. The policies are specified by the Archive Manager, developed in collaboration with the Archivist, implemented by the IT staff, and applied by the Archive admin. Each policy controls the execution of a procedure that is defined as a workflow composed from basic functions, called micro-services. Note that both the policies and the micro-services may evolve over time, and need to be registered into the metadata catalog. The policies and procedures are registered into the data grid catalog. A report can be generated by retrieving the rules and micro-services from the catalog and writing a report.

Property Management: If a policy exists for each task, then the duties are well established. However the tasks may evolve and additional policies may be needed over time. To track evolution of the policies and micro-services:

- Policy16 – rac-registerPolicies.r

  ◦ Register a policy into the data grid. Note that policies can be versioned. The rule is assumed to be contained in a text file, and is registered into the metadata catalog in collection GLOBAL_ACCOUNT/GLOBAL_REPOSITORY/GLOBAL_RULES. The action is logged in Archive-RAA.

- Policy17 – rac-registerMicroservices.r

  ◦ Register a micro-service into the data grid. Note that micro-services are plugged into the middleware framework. The metadata catalog can be used to maintain a list of the registered micro-services in collection GLOBAL_ACCOUNT/GLOBAL_REPOSITORY/GLOBAL_RULES. The action is logged in Archive-RAA.

Property Assessment: Retrieve the most recent versions of the policies and micro-services and generate an Archive-PPRS document that lists the active preservation policies. This document will need to be managed with Policy3-Policy8, Policy26, Policy35, and Policy36.

- Policy18 – rac-listPolicies.r

  ◦ Retrieve the most recent version of the policies and list their names in the report Archive-PPRS stored in GLOBAL_ACCOUNT/GLOBAL_REPOSITORY/GLOBAL_REPORTS.

- Policy19 – rac-listMicroservices.r

    ° Retrieve the names of the micro-services and save them in the report Archive-PMA, stored in
    GLOBAL_ACCOUNT/GLOBAL_REPOSITORY/GLOBAL_REPORTS.

3.3.2.1 *The repository shall have mechanisms for review, update, and ongoing development of its Preservation Policies as the repository grows and as technology and community practice evolve.*

The data grid middleware is based on a pluggable framework. New policies, new procedures, and new technologies can be plugged into the framework dynamically. The middleware uses two levels of indirection to ensure that the archive properties can be maintained when new technologies are plugged in. The middleware maps actions specified by clients to operations specified by micro-services and then maps the micro-service operations to the protocol required by each technology. Thus the policies do not have to be modified as new technologies are incorporated into the system. The properties are enforced by procedures that are written in the iRODS rule language.

However the community practice can evolve and require construction of additional policies to enforce new properties. A process for updating the Preservation Policies is defined in the Preservation Implementation Plan (Archive-PIP) that consists of the following steps.

1. Identify the preservation properties currently implemented. These properties are saved as metadata attributes on the archive collection, archive files, and staff.

    ° Policy20 – rac-listAttributes.r

        - Retrieve a list of attributes associated with the preservation properties and store in Archive-PMRA in the collection
        GLOBAL_ACCOUNT/*Archive/GLOBAL_REPORTS.

2. The Archive Manager and Archivist define the new properties and policies that are needed.

3. The policies are implemented by the IT staff.

4. The policies are registered into the metadata catalog, along with new versions of micro-services. The policies are stored in
GLOBAL_ACCOUNT/GLOBAL_REPOSITORY/GLOBAL_RULES. Versions of the policies are stored in
GLOBAL_ACCOUNT/GLOBAL_REPOSITORY/GLOBAL_RULES/GLOBAL_VERSIONS.

    ° Policy16 – rac-registerPolicies.r

- Register a policy into the data grid. Note that policies will be versioned by this rule. The rule is assumed to be contained in a text file, and is located on the repository administrator's server. The action is logged in Archive-RAA.

4.1. Policy17 – rac-registerMicroservices.r

4.4.1. Register a micro-service into the data grid. Note that micro-services are plugged into the middleware framework. The metadata catalog can be used to maintain a list of the registered micro-services. The action is logged in Archive-RAA.

5. The Preservation Policies are periodically reviewed.

  ○ Policy6 – rac-generateReportNotifications.r

    - Maintain a manifest, Archive-NPRA, of e-mail notifications for management review. Send notifications each year for updates to a specified plan.

The Preservation Implementation Plan (Archive-PIP) is managed by Policy3-Policy8, Policy26, Policy35, and Policy36 and is stored in GLOBAL_ACCOUNT/GLOBAL_REPOSITORY/GLOBAL_REPORTS.

The report contains:

Operations – Documentation of plan reviews
Operations – Documentation of review cycles for documentation of plans
Operations – Plans for on-going development of preservation policies
Operations – Plans for policies to handle technology changes
Operations – Plans for policies to track community practice evolution

A second document, Technology/Community Report (Archive-TC), is needed to manage surveys of the community to track their current requirements and practices. The Technology/Community Report is managed by Policy3-Policy8, Policy26, Policy35, and Policy36, and is stored in GLOBAL_ACCOUNT/GLOBAL_REPOSITORY/GLOBAL_REPORTS.

The report contains:

Archives – Surveys of community practice
Operations – Surveys of technology changes

A third document is a copy of the current rule base, stored as the document Archive-PPA. The Archive-PPA report documents the current set of rules that are being enforced by the repository. The Preservation Policies Report is managed by Policy3-Policy8, Policy26, Policy35, and Policy36 and is stored in GLOBAL_ACCOUNT/GLOBAL_REPOSITORY/GLOBAL_REPORTS.

Property Management:

- Policy25 – rac-listRulebase.r

  ○ List the policies in the rule base in Archive-PPA and generate a versioned report that will be publicly accessible. The report is stored in GLOBAL_ACCOUNT/GLOBAL_REPOSITORY/GLOBAL_REPORTS.

3.3.3   THE REPOSITORY SHALL HAVE A DOCUMENTED HISTORY OF THE CHANGES TO ITS OPERATIONS, PROCEDURES, SOFTWARE, AND HARDWARE

As new technologies are added to the preservation system, the data grid middleware automatically creates a pre- and post-process policy enforcement point for controlling interactions. The use of the technology can be audited, with an event posted to an external indexing system, such as Elastic Search. The indexing system can be queried to track changes to the environment, events related to archives management, and enforcement of preservation properties.

The audit events can report the version number of the policy, micro-services, and plug-ins that are used. Note that auditing can be implemented as a meta-rule that is applied first before the policy associated with the plug-in is applied.

Property Creation:

- Policy16 – rac-registerPolicies.r

  ○ A copy of an audit rule is stored in GLOBAL_ACCOUNT/GLOBAL_REPOSITORY/GLOBAL_RULES.

- Policy21 – rac-setAuditEvents.r

  ○ Add an audit meta-rule for recording the version number of the policy, micro-service, or plug-in that is being accessed. The action is logged in Archive-RAA.

Property Assessment:

- Policy81 – rac-listAuditEventInfrastructure.r

  ○ Query the external indexing system to retrieve a list of the audit events, the date, and the technology that was used for a specified time interval. Store the results

in Archive-IRA in collection
GLOBAL_ACCOUNT/*Archive/GLOBAL_REPORTS.

A document on Infrastructure Acquisition, Archive-IA, describes the capital equipment. The report is externally generated and is stored in GLOBAL_ACCOUNT/GLOBAL_REPOSITORY/GLOBAL_REPORTS. The report contains:

Archives – Capital equipment inventory
Archives – History of acquisition, implementation, update and retirement of software and hardware
Operations – File retention and disposition schedules
Operations – Copies of prior policies and procedures
Operations – Minutes of meetings

3.3.4   THE REPOSITORY SHALL COMMIT TO TRANSPARENCY AND ACCOUNTABILITY IN ALL ACTIONS SUPPORTING THE OPERATION AND MANAGEMENT OF THE REPOSITORY THAT AFFECT THE PRESERVATION OF DIGITAL CONTENT OVER TIME

A technical audit report (Archive-TAR) is generated periodically and contains:

Operations – Technical audits
Operations – Technical certifications
Repository – Contracts and agreements with critical service providers
Repository – Contracts and agreements with funding providers
Repository – Documentation of governance requirements
Repository – Financial certifications
Repository – Independent program reviews

The Technical Audit Report is managed by Policy3-Policy8, Policy26, Policy35, and Policy36, and is stored in GLOBAL_ACCOUNT/GLOBAL_REPOSITORY/GLOBAL_REPORTS.

The reports listed in Table 2.3 are made publicly accessible by assigning an access permission for the "anonymous" account to the "GLOBAL_REPOSITORY" collection, and turning on inheritance. This ensures that all reports can be read, including the yearly versions.

The rules that query audit trails are also made publicly accessible, by loading them into a "GLOBAL_RULES" sub-collection under the "GLOBAL_REPOSITORY" collection.

Property Creation:

- Policy23 – rac-setPublicAccess.r

    ○ The rule sets public access to the GLOBAL_REPOSITORY collection. The action is logged in Archive-RAA.

Property Assessment:

- Policy24 – rac-verifyPublicAccess.r

    ○ The rule verifies that the GLOBAL_REPOSITORY collection has inheritance set and has public access set. The action is logged in Archive-RAA.

3.3.5   THE REPOSITORY SHALL DEFINE, COLLECT, TRACK, AND APPROPRIATELY PROVIDE ITS INFORMATION INTEGRITY MEASUREMENTS

The policies that enforce integrity are documented in the Archive-PPA Preservation Policies document.

Information integrity is enabled by generating checksums, replicating the information, and periodically verifying the integrity of the checksums. The integrity of the metadata catalog is equally important, and is achieved through replication of the catalog and the periodic creation of database dumps. An example of a process to replicate the catalog is to use PostgreSQL streaming replication. This periodically ships XLOG records generated by the primary database to a standby database. The standby database continually replays the XLOG records to ensure that the standby database mirrors the primary database.

A checksum using the SHA-256 standard is generated by Policy26, rac-setChecksum.re, when a file is loaded into the archive. The checksum is saved in the persistent state attribute DATA_CHECKSUM associated with each file. Each file is replicated automatically, by using a replication resource. An example replication resource is constructed using a storage hierarchy, as shown for the SILS LifeTime Library.

```
LTLResc:passthru
└── LTLRepl:replication
        ├── LTLRenci:unix file system
        └── LTLSils:unix file system
```

The top level of the storage hierarchy is a pass through node, called LTLResc. This is used to allow the lower level nodes in the storage hierarchy to be changed without affecting the controlling policies. The next level in the storage hierarchy is a replication node. This controls the replication of the file onto all leaf nodes, in this case LTLRenci and LTLSils. The two leaf nodes are at two different physical locations, and use different types of storage systems to minimize risk of data loss.

Property Creation:

- Policy26 – rac-setChecksum.re

   ○ The rule generates a checksum for each deposited file. It is implemented as an extension to Policy2, rac-setReportUpdateDate.re, and is applied at the acPostProcForPut policy enforcement point. The micro-service

      msiDataObjChksum($objPath, "forceChksum=", *Chksum);

   is executed after the file is stored. The policy is applied to files deposited into GLOBAL_ACCOUNT/GLOBAL_REPOSITORY/GLOBAL_REPORTS and into GLOBAL_ACCOUNT/*Archive/GLOBAL_REPORTS.

Property Assessment:

- Policy27 – rac-checkNumberReplicas.r

   ○ The rule checks that the required number of replicas exist for each file. A replica check report called Archive-RCA is updated and stored in GLOBAL_ACCOUNT/GLOBAL_REPOSITORY/MANIFESTS.

- Policy28 – rac-updateReplicas.r

   ○ The rule forces a rebalance operation to ensure that the leaf nodes of the replication resource each contain a replica. The action is logged in Archive-RAA.

- Policy29 – rac-verifyIntegrity.r

   ○ The rule verifies the checksum of each file in the *Archive collections. This is a lengthy process that may be done yearly. Errors that are found are documented in the manifest Archive-RCA, and each corrupted file is replaced with a good copy.

3.3.6   THE REPOSITORY SHALL COMMIT TO A REGULAR SCHEDULE OF SELF-ASSESSMENT AND EXTERNAL CERTIFICATION

The Certification Report, Archive-CR, is a management report that is generated externally by the management team. The report documents the audits and certifications of compliance with ISO Standards.

The report contains:

Repository – Certificates awarded for compliance with relevant ISO standards	
Repository – Completed and dated checklists from self-assessments	
Repository – Completed and dated checklists from third-party audits	
Repository – Timetables and evidence of adequate budget allocations for future certifications	

The Certification Report is managed by Policy3-Policy8, Policy26, Policy35, and Policy36 and is stored in GLOBAL_ACCOUNT/GLOBAL_REPOSITORY/GLOBAL_REPORTS.

3.4   FINANCIAL SUSTAINABILITY

The documents that describe the financial sustainability are described in Section 3.4.

Business Planning report	Archive-BPR	ISO 3.4.1
Budget report	Archive-BR	ISO 3.4.2
Financial Audit report	Archive-FAR	ISO 3.4.2
Financial Risk report	Archive-FR	ISO 3.4.3

3.4.1   THE REPOSITORY SHALL HAVE SHORT- AND LONG-TERM BUSINESS PLANNING PROCESSES IN PLACE TO SUSTAIN THE REPOSITORY OVER TIME

The Business Planning Report, Archive-BPR, is a management report that is generated externally by the management team. The report documents the short- and long-term business planning processes. The report contains:

Operations – Documentation of current operating plans
Operations – Plans for multi-year strategic operation
Repository – Documentation of current business practices
Repository – Documentation of market Analysis
Repository – Financial forecasts with multiple budget scenarios
Repository – Plans for contingencies
Repository – Plans for multi-year business strategy

The Business Planning Report is managed by Policy3-Policy8, Policy26, Policy35, and Policy36 and is stored in GLOBAL_ACCOUNT/GLOBAL_REPOSITORY/GLOBAL_REPORTS.

3.4.2 THE REPOSITORY SHALL HAVE FINANCIAL PRACTICES AND PROCEDURES WHICH ARE TRANSPARENT, COMPLIANT WITH RELEVANT ACCOUNTING STANDARDS AND PRACTICES, AND AUDITED BY THIRD PARTIES IN ACCORDANCE WITH TERRITORIAL LEGAL REQUIREMENTS

The Budget Report, Archive-BR, is a management report that is generated externally by the management team. The report documents the financial practices and procedures.

The report contains:

Operations – Documentation of requirements for accounting and auditing
Repository – Documentation of standards for accounting and auditing
Repository – Plans for evolution of business practices

The Budget Report is managed by Policy3-Policy8, Policy26, Policy35, and Policy36 and is stored in
GLOBAL_ACCOUNT/GLOBAL_REPOSITORY/GLOBAL_REPORTS.

The financial practices are audited by third parties, and documented in the Financial Audit Report, Archive-FAR. The Financial Audit Report contains:

Repository – Financial statement audits

The Financial Audit Report is managed by Policy3-Policy8, Policy26, Policy35, and Policy36 and is stored in
GLOBAL_ACCOUNT/GLOBAL_REPOSITORY/GLOBAL_REPORTS.

3.4.3 THE REPOSITORY SHALL HAVE AN ONGOING COMMITMENT TO ANALYZE AND REPORT ON RISK, BENEFIT, INVESTMENT, AND EXPENDITURE (INCLUDING ASSETS, LICENSES, AND LIABILITIES)

The Financial Risk Report, Archive-FR, defines the risk and benefit of investments. The report is generated by the management team, and is managed using Policy3-Policy8, Policy26, Policy35, and Policy36. The report is stored in
GLOBAL_ACCOUNT/GLOBAL_REPOSITORY/GLOBAL_REPORTS.

Repository – Identify perceived and potential financial risks and plan responses
Repository – Technology infrastructure investment planning
Repository – Cost/benefit analyses
Repository – Financial investment documents and portfolios

| Repository – Licenses, contracts, and requirements for asset management |
| Repository – History of changes based on risk |

3.5   CONTRACTS, LICENSES, AND LIABILITIES

The documents that describe contracts, licenses, and liabilities are described in Section 3.5.

Service Level Agreement report	Archive-SL	ISO 3.5.1
Deposit Agreement report (metadata)	Archive-DAR	ISO 3.5.1.1
Submission Agreement report	Archive-SAR	ISO 3.5.1.2
Standard Operating Procedure	Archive-SOP	ISO 3.5.1.2
Confirmation report	Archive-CFR	ISO 3.5.1.3
Access list	Archive-ALRA	ISO 3.5.1.4
Disputed Data set report	Archive-DD	ISO 3.5.1.4
Disputed Data set audit	Archive-DIDA	ISO 3.5.1.4
Intellectual Property report	Archive-IP	ISO 3.5.2
Intellectual Property audit	Archive-IPA	ISO 3.5.2

3.5.1   THE REPOSITORY SHALL HAVE AND MAINTAIN APPROPRIATE CONTRACTS OR DEPOSIT AGREEMENTS FOR DIGITAL MATERIALS THAT IT MANAGES, PRESERVES, AND/OR TO WHICH IT PROVIDES ACCESS

Interactions with each provider of archives material is managed by a Service Level Agreement, Archive-SL. This documents the permissions needed by the repository to collect and preserve digital content. A separate document is negotiated with each producer of archives material. The document contains:

| Archives – Agreements for service level definitions |
| Archives – Deposit licenses |
| Archives – Documentation of permitted uses |
| Archives – Policies for review and maintenance of documents |
| Archives – Policies for third-party deposit arrangements |
| Archives – Policies for treatment of orphan works and copyright dispute resolution |
| Operations – History of risk assessment reports from independent review |

The report is managed by Policy3-Policy8, Policy26, Policy35, and Policy36, and is stored in GLOBAL_ACCOUNT/*Archive/GLOBAL_REPORTS.

3.5.1.1 The repository shall have contracts or deposit agreements which specify and transfer all necessary preservation rights, and those rights transferred shall be documented.

A separate deposit agreement, Archive-DAR, is required from each producer. The document is generated externally and managed within the repository by Policy3-Policy8, Policy26, Policy35, and Policy36. The report is stored in GLOBAL_ACCOUNT/*Archive/GLOBAL_REPORTS.

The document includes:

Archives – Agreements for deposit (signed and executed)
Archives – Contracts
Archives – Documentation of rights, licenses, and permissions obtained from producers
Archives – Policies for preservation rights

3.5.1.2 The repository shall have specified all appropriate aspects of acquisition, maintenance, access, and withdrawal in written agreements with depositors and other relevant parties.

A separate submission agreement, Archive-SAR, is required from each producer. The document is generated externally and managed within the repository by Policy3-Policy8, Policy26, Policy35, and Policy36. The report is stored in GLOBAL_ACCOUNT/*Archive/GLOBAL_REPORTS.

The document includes:

Archives – Agreements for access
Archives – Agreements for Submission (properly executed)
Archives – Agreements for Withdrawal
Archives – Deeds of gifts

The aggregate of the submission agreements should be combined into a Standard Operating Procedure that provides the basic management procedures across all archives. The document, Archive-SOP, is stored in GLOBAL_ACCOUNT/GLOBAL_REPOSITORY/GLOBAL_REPORTS and contains:

Operations – Documentation of standard operating procedures

3.5.1.3 The repository shall have written policies that indicate when it accepts preservation responsibility for contents of each set of submitted data objects.

A separate confirmation report, Archive-CFR, is required from each producer to document the transfer of responsibility. The document is generated externally and managed within the repository by Policy3-Policy8, Policy26, Policy35, and Policy36. The report is stored in GLOBAL_ACCOUNT/*Archive/GLOBAL_REPORTS.
    The document includes:

Archives – Agreements for confirming Receipt for responsibility for digital objects

3.5.1.4 The repository shall have policies in place to address liability and challenges to ownership/ rights.

A separate report, Archive-DD, is required from each producer to document the policies and procedures for resolving disputes related to ownership and liability. The document is generated externally and managed within the repository by Policy3-Policy8, Policy26, Policy35, and Policy36. The report is stored in GLOBAL_ACCOUNT/*Archive/GLOBAL_REPORTS.
    The document includes:

Operations – Policies for responding to challenges
Repository – Documentation of citations to relevant laws and regulations
Repository – Documentation of records of relevant legal advice

A second document is generated dynamically to identify all disputes for each archives. A query is made to an external auditing system to identify disputed access, and the results are stored in a file called Archive-DIDA in collection GLOBAL_ACCOUNT/*Archive/GLOBAL_REPORTS. The report contains information for:

Archives – Documentation of disputed data set events and resolution

Relevant policies are:
Property Creation:

- Policy21 – rac-setAuditEvents.r

    ○ Set an audit meta-rule for recording access events. The action is logged in Archive-RAA.

- Policy30 – rac-removeAccess.r

       ◦ Remove access for a specified account to an archives. All changes are logged to a manifest file, Archive-ALRA, the Access report, which is stored in GLOBAL_ACCOUNT/*Archive/GLOBAL_MANIFESTS.

- Policy31 – rac-setAccess.r

       ◦ Set access for a specified account to an archives. All changes are logged to a manifest file, Archive-ALRA, the Access report, which is stored in GLOBAL_ACCOUNT/*Archive/GLOBAL_MANIFESTS.

Property Assessment:

- Policy22 – rac-listAuditEvents.r

       ◦ Query the external indexing system to retrieve a list of the audit events, the date, and the person who accessed the data for disputed data. Store the versioned report in Archive-DIDA in collection GLOBAL_ACCOUNT/*Archive/GLOBAL_REPORTS.

- Policy32 – rac-listAccess.r

       ◦ Generate a list of persons who have access permission to an archives. The list is written to Access report, Archive-ALRA, which is stored in GLOBAL_ACCOUNT/*Archive/GLOBAL_MANIFESTS.

3.5.2   THE REPOSITORY SHALL TRACK AND MANAGE INTELLECTUAL PROPERTY RIGHTS AND RESTRICTIONS ON USE OF REPOSITORY CONTENT AS REQUIRED BY DEPOSIT AGREEMENT, CONTRACT, OR LICENSE

A separate report, Archive-IP, is required from each producer to document the intellectual property rights for an archives. The document is generated externally and managed within the repository by Policy3-Policy8, Policy26, Policy35, and Policy36. The report is stored in GLOBAL_ACCOUNT/*Archive/GLOBAL_REPORTS.

The document includes:

Archives – Agreements for managing intellectual property rights
Archives – Audit of changes to intellectual property
Archives – Documentation of metadata that captures rights information
Archives – Documentation of requirements for managing intellectual property rights
Archives – Policies for enforcing intellectual property rights

A second document is generated as a manifest file that records changes to the Intellectual Property Rights, Archive-IPA. A metadata attribute, Archive-IPR, is added to the *Archive collections to specify a person as the owner of the Intellectual Property. If the field is null, public access is allowed. If the Archive-IPR attribute contains an account name, then access is restricted to that account.

Property Creation:

- Policy33- rac-setIPR.r

  ○ Set IPR owner for collections as metadata attribute on an *Archive collection as a value of the Archive-IPR attribute. The action is logged to Archive-IPA.

Property Management:

- Policy34 – rac-resetIPR.r

  ○ Remove non-compatible access controls from an *Archive collection, and generate a manifest file, Archive-IPA, that records the changes. The report is stored in GLOBAL_ACCOUNT/*Archive/GLOBAL_MANIFESTS.

Property Assessment:

- Policy37 – rac-verifyIPR.r

  ○ Verify access controls on an *Archive collection are compatible with the IPR owner. Document incompatible access controls in a manifest file, Archive-IPA. The report is stored in GLOBAL_ACCOUNT/*Archive/GLOBAL_MANIFESTS.

CHAPTER 4

ISO 16363 Digital Object Management

Section 4 of the ISO 16363 standard specifies the tasks required to manage submission of content, creation of Archival Information Packages, and creation of Dissemination Information Packages.

Many of the documents that provide information to funders, depositors, and users about the information properties that the repository will preserve have been described by criteria defined in Chapter 3. These documents include:

Mission statement	Archive-MS	ISO 3.1.1
Collection policy report	Archive-CollP	ISO 3.1.3
Designated community report	Archive-DCP	ISO 3.3.1
Preservation policies	Archive-PPA	ISO 3.3.2
Policy metadata report	Archive-PMRA	ISO 3.3.2.1
Preservation implementation plan	Archive-PIP	ISO 3.3.2.1
Service level agreement report	Archive-SL	ISO 3.5.1
Deposit agreement report	Archive-DAR	ISO 3.5.1.1
Submission agreement report	Archive-SAR	ISO 3.5.1.2
Intellectual property report	Archive-IP	ISO 3.5.2

4.1 INGEST: ACQUISITION OF CONTENT

A standard task on acquisition is verification that the information content is sufficient to implement the preservation information properties. Two documents have already been defined in Chapter 3.

Standard Operating Procedures Documents processing steps	Archive-SOP	ISO 3.5.1.2
Confirmation report Documents the receipt of SIPS	Archive-CFR	ISO 3.5.1.3

Additional documents about the information properties of the repository that are discussed in Section 4.1 include:

Authenticity requirements report	Archive-AU	ISO 4.1.1.1
Information properties report	Archive-INP	ISO 4.1.1
Content information report	Archive-CID	ISO 4.1.2
SIP submission requirements report	Archive-SSR	ISO 4.1.3
SIP template	Archive-SIP	ISO 4.1.3

4.1.1 THE REPOSITORY SHALL IDENTIFY THE CONTENT INFORMATION AND THE INFORMATION PROPERTIES THAT THE REPOSITORY WILL PRESERVE

Each archives may independently specify required information. The properties are documented in an externally created Information Properties report, Archive-INP, that defines the metadata attributes associated with each collection and each file. The metadata may be registered as attributes on the collections and files, or may be encapsulated in an XML or JSON file and stored as separate files. The Information Properties report, Archive-INP, is managed within the repository by Policy3-Policy8, Policy26, Policy35, and Policy36 and is stored in the collection GLOBAL_ACCOUNT/*Archive/GLOBAL_REPORTS.

The specific information properties that are preserved for each archives are encapsulated in metadata associated with the GLOBAL_ACCOUNT/*Archive collections.

The report Archive-INP defines the required information properties, and the report Archive-PMRA lists the actual preserved information properties.

The Archive-INP document contains:

Archives – Requirements for Responsibilities for records
Archives – Requirements for Processing procedures for records
Archives – Requirements for Preserved information properties

Policy20 lists the actual preservation metadata attributes that are managed by the repository and stores the list in the Policy Metadata Report, Archive-PMRA, in the collection GLOBAL_ACCOUNT/*Archive/GLOBAL_REPORTS.

Property Management:

• Policy20 – rac-listAttributes.r

  ○ Retrieve a list of attributes associated with the preservation information properties and store in Archive-PMRA.

4.1.1.1 The repository shall have a procedure(s) for identifying those Information Properties that it will preserve.

The authenticity of the records in a repository is verified through analysis of the preserved information properties. Examples of properties that should be preserved over time include:

- Provenance information documenting the source of records in a collection. This can be preserved as a source attribute assigned to records in the *Archive collection.

    ○ Audit-Source

- Integrity information such as replicas and checksums. These attributes are managed by the data grid for each record and include:

    ○ DATA_REPL_NUM   data replica number

    ○ DATA_PATH   data storage path

    ○ DATA_CHECKSUM   data checksum

- Representation information documenting the record format type and the Designated Community. The format type is managed in the attribute

    ○ DATA_TYPE_NAME

    The name of the Designated Community ontology is preserved as a source attribute assigned to *Archive

    ○ Archive-Ontology

- Chain of custody, documenting the management and storage decisions. This is maintained as an audit trail that tracks all file creation events for date and location. Additional information is stored in reports:

Authenticity requirements report	Archive-AU	ISO 4.1.1.1
Integrity Report	Archive-INTA	ISO 4.2.9
Access log	Archive-ALA	ISO 4.6.1
Traceability report (operations/state)	Archive-TRA	ISO 5.1.1.6

The authenticity requirements report, Archive-AU, documents

Archives – Policies for processing digital objects
Operations – Policies for auditing events
Operations – Policies for tracking chain of custody

and is managed within the repository by Policy3-Policy8, Policy35, and Policy36. Archive-AU is stored in
GLOBAL_ACCOUNT/*Archive/GLOBAL_REPORTS.

4.1.1.2 *The repository shall have a record of the Content Information and the Information Properties that it will preserve.*

The documents that identify commitments include:

Preservation Policies	Archive-PPA	ISO 3.3.2
Preservation Implementation Plan	Archive-PIP	ISO 3.3.2.1
Authenticity Requirements	Archive-AU	ISO 4.1.1.1
Content Information Deposition report	Archive-CIRA	ISO 4.1.1.2

The Content Information Deposition report, Archive-CIRA, is a survey of an archives, listing the number of files that have been archived, the storage size, the types of files, and the most recent deposition date by sub-collection. The Archive-CIRA report is generated by Policy38, rac-surveyArchive.r.

Property Management:

- Policy38 – rac-surveyArchive.r

    ○ Analyze GLOBAL_ACCOUNT/*Archive/GLOBAL_ARCHIVES to survey the contents. Generate metrics for size, number of files, types of files, and most recent deposition. The report, Archive-CIRA, is stored in GLOBAL_ACCOUNT/*Archive/GLOBAL_REPORTS.

4.1.2   THE REPOSITORY SHALL CLEARLY SPECIFY THE INFORMATION THAT NEEDS TO BE ASSOCIATED WITH SPECIFIC CONTENT INFORMATION AT THE TIME OF ITS DEPOSIT

The information required on submission is specified by a producer-archive transfer agreement, documented in Archive-CID. This report is stored in the GLOBAL_ACCOUNT/*Archive/GLOBAL_REPORTS collection. The document contains:

Archives – Agreements for Producer-archive transfer
Archives – Requirements for information associated with content
Archives – Transfer requirements

The Archive-CID document is managed by Policy3-Policy8, Policy26, Policy35, and Policy36.

4.1.3 THE REPOSITORY SHALL HAVE ADEQUATE SPECIFICATIONS ENABLING RECOGNITION AND PARSING OF THE SIPS

The structure of the Submission Information Package is defined in the template, Archive-SIP. This document is stored in the GLOBAL_ACCOUNT/*Archive/GLOBAL_REPORTS collection. The format of the template may be JSON, or XML, or CSV.

The Archive-SIP document specifies:

Archives – Packaging Information for the SIPs
Archives – Required provenance metadata attribute names
Archives – Required descriptive metadata attribute names
Archives – Required representation metadata attribute names
Archives – Required intellectual property ownership names
Archives – Required access control names
Archives – Required Designated Community ontology name

In this paper, the Archive-SIP document is structured as a list of pipe-delimited metadata attributes. Each required piece of information is given an attribute name, an attribute value, and an attribute comment field. The attributes are assigned to the collection GLOBAL_ACCOUNT/*Archive/GLOBAL_SIPS.

The format is:

C-collection_name | attribute_name | attribute_value | attribute_comment

The attribute_name, attribute_value, and attribute_comment are stored as a triplet called an AVU and assigned as metadata on the specified collection_name.

An example Archive-SIP document contains:

```
C-/lifelibZone/home/rwmoore/Archive-A/SIPS |Audit-Depositor |RequiredSIP |
C-/lifelibZone/home/rwmoore/Archive-A/SIPS |Audit-Source |RequiredSIP |
C-/lifelibZone/home/rwmoore/Archive-A/SIPS |Archive-Format |RequiredSIP |
C-/lifelibZone/home/rwmoore/Archive-A/SIPS |Archive-IPR |RequiredSIP |
C-/lifelibZone/home/rwmoore/Archive-A/SIPS |Archive-Ontology |RequiredSIP |
C-/lifelibZone/home/rwmoore/Archive-A/SIPS |Archive-Description |RequiredSIP |
```

where the required SIP attributes are given the value of "RequiredSIP".

The Archive-SIP document is managed by Policy3-Policy8, Policy26, Policy35, and Policy36.

Additional information is provided in the document Archive-SSR which defines the SIP Submission Requirements. This document defines:

Archives – Documentation of file format specifications
Archives – Documentation of published data standards
Archives – Documentation of representation information for the SIP Content Data
Operations – Documentation of valid object construction

The document Archive-SSR is stored in GLOBAL_ACCOUNT/*Archive/GLOBAL_REPORTS and is managed by Policy3-Policy8, Policy26, Policy35, and Policy36.

4.1.4   THE REPOSITORY SHALL HAVE MECHANISMS TO APPROPRIATELY VERIFY THE DEPOSITOR OF ALL MATERIALS

The persistent state attribute, Audit-Depositor. can be set for each SIP that is deposited into GLOBAL_ACCOUNT/*Archive/GLOBAL_SIPS.

Property Creation:

- Policy39- rac-setSource.r

  - Set the depositor for a SIP using the metadata attribute Audit-Depositor and set the source for a SIP using the metadata attribute Audit-Source. The value of the Audit-Depositor attribute is the name of the depositor. The value of the Audit-Source attribute may be the project or institution name. The action is logged in Archive-PAA.

Property Assessment:

- Policy40 – rac-verifySource.r

  - Verify that the depositor and the source have been defined for each SIP. SIPs that are missing information are listed in the manifest Archive-CINCA, stored in the collection GLOBAL_ACCOUNT/*Archive/GLOBAL_REPORTS. The policy checks all attributes specified in a list. Additional attributes can be added to the list by modifying the policy.

4.1.5 THE REPOSITORY SHALL HAVE AN INGEST PROCESS WHICH VERIFIES EACH SIP FOR COMPLETENESS AND CORRECTNESS

Each Submission Information Package should be checked for errors. This includes creation errors and transmission errors. While the document Archive-SIP defines the required preservation information, a second document Archive-META is used to ingest required metadata preservation information and assign the information as attributes on the GLOBAL_SIPS collection. Note that Archive-META and Archive-SIP should contain the same information. However, if the standard for the preservation metadata is changed, then Archive-SIP may represent the new version. Changes can be made to the GLOBAL_SIPS collection attributes using a version of Archive-META that only contains the updates.

The required preservation information may be formatted as XML or as a pipe-delimited file, and is stored in GLOBAL_ACCOUNT/*Archive/GLOBAL_REPORTS/Archive-META. The Archive-META file is parsed to assign the required preservation metadata attributes to the GLOBAL_ACCOUNT/*Archive/GLOBAL_SIPS collection. An example Archive-META file contains:

```
C-/lifelibZone/home/rwmoore/Archive-A/SIPS |Audit-Depositor |RequiredSIP |
C-/lifelibZone/home/rwmoore/Archive-A/SIPS |Audit-Source |RequiredSIP |
C-/lifelibZone/home/rwmoore/Archive-A/SIPS |Archive-Format |RequiredSIP |
C-/lifelibZone/home/rwmoore/Archive-A/SIPS |Archive-IPR |RequiredSIP |
C-/lifelibZone/home/rwmoore/Archive-A/SIPS |Archive-Ontology |RequiredSIP |
C-/lifelibZone/home/rwmoore/Archive-A/SIPS |Archive-Description |RequiredSIP |
  |
```

Note that each attribute name registered onto the GLOBAL_SIPS collection is given an attribute value of "RequiredSIP". This is done to make it possible to differentiate between metadata required for SIPs versus metadata required for AIPs.

Integrity properties are automatically handled by the data grid. Depending upon the ingestion method, a checksum is created before the file is transmitted, and verified upon receipt. Policy26, rac-setChecksum.re, generates a checksum after the file has been ingested.

Required representation information (such as file type, or knowledge ontology) can also be captured as attributes in the auxiliary metadata file, Archive-META, which is stored in GLOBAL_ACCOUNT/*Archive/GLOBAL_REPORTS.

Property Creation:

- Policy41 – rac-setMetadata.r

  ○ Read a pipe-delimited metadata file and set the required SIP metadata attributes on a specified collection name. The format of the file is

```
C-/lifelibZone/home/rwmoore/Archive-A/SIPS |Audit-Depositor |RequiredSIP |
C-/lifelibZone/home/rwmoore/Archive-A/SIPS |Audit-Source |RequiredSIP |
```

```
C-/lifelibZone/home/rwmoore/Archive-A/SIPS |Archive-Format |RequiredSIP |
C-/lifelibZone/home/rwmoore/Archive-A/SIPS |Archive-IPR |RequiredSIP |
C-/lifelibZone/home/rwmoore/Archive-A/SIPS |Archive-Ontology |RequiredSIP |
C-/lifelibZone/home/rwmoore/Archive-A/SIPS |Archive-Description |RequiredSIP |
C-/lifelibZone/home/rwmoore/Archive-A/SIPS |Archive-CheckVirus |1 |
C-/lifelibZone/home/rwmoore/Archive-A/SIPS |Archive-CheckProtected |1 |
C-/lifelibZone/home/rwmoore/Archive-A/SIPS |Archive-CheckFormat |1 |
C-/lifelibZone/home/rwmoore/Archive-A/SIPS |Archive-CheckMetadata |1 |
C-/lifelibZone/home/rwmoore/Archive-A/SIPS |Archive-CheckVocab |1 |
C-/lifelibZone/home/rwmoore/Archive-A/SIPS |Archive-CheckIntegrity |1 |
C-/lifelibZone/home/rwmoore/Archive-A/SIPS |Archive-CheckDup |1 |
```

The file is located in GLOBAL_ACCOUNT/*Archive/GLOBAL_REPORTS and is called Archive-META. Note that processing control attributes, such as Archive-CheckVirus, can also be set. When the value is "1", the processing step is applied on conversion of SIPs to AIPs. See Policy 51, rac-checkSIP.r.

- Policy42- rac-inputMetadata.r

  ○ Read pipe-delimited metadata files and load the attributes onto a SIP. A standard name for the metadata file is the record name with "-meta" appended. The format of the file is

  ```
  /lifelibZone/home/rwmoore/Archive-A/SIPS/rec3 |Audit-Depositor |rwmoore |
  /lifelibZone/home/rwmoore/Archive-A/SIPS/rec3 |Audit-Source |DFC |
  ```

  This example adds SIP attributes to a SIP called "rec3" from a metadata file that resides in the GLOBAL_ACCOUNT/*Archive/GLOBAL_METADATA directory. The value of Audit-Depositor is set to "rwmoore". The value of Audit-Source is set to "DFC".

  In this example policy, a list is made of all of the files in GLOBAL_ACCOUNT/*Archive/GLOBAL_METADATA. Each metadata file that is found is processed. Note that a separate metadata file can be stored for each record, or all of the metadata information can be aggregated into a single file. Only files whose names end in "-meta" are parsed.

  The attributes that are specified in the metadata file are loaded onto the SIP specified within the metadata file. The action is logged in Archive-SIPCRA.

Property Assessment:
- Policy43 – rac-verifyMetadata.r

○ This policy may be used to verify either required information for SIPs or required information for AIPs. Set the input *Type to "SIPS" for verifying SIPs or to "AIPS" for verifying AIPs.

The attributes that are registered on the GLOBAL_SIPS collection that have a value of "RequiredSIP" are compared with the attributes registered on each file in the GLOBAL_SIPS collection. A report is generated of the missing attributes called Archive-SIPCRA, which is stored in GLOBAL_ACCOUNT/*Archive/GLOBAL_MANIFESTS.

For AIPs, the attributes that are registered on the GLOBAL_ARCHIVES collection that have a value of "RequiredAIP" are compared with the attributes registered on each file in the GLOBAL_ARCHIVES collection. A report is generated of the missing attributes called Archive-AIPCRA, which is stored in GLOBAL_ACCOUNT/*Archive/GLOBAL_MANIFESTS.

4.1.6 THE REPOSITORY SHALL OBTAIN SUFFICIENT CONTROL OVER THE DIGITAL OBJECTS TO PRESERVE THEM

Control of digital objects requires the ability to:

• Maintain a persistent name for each record

• Maintain information about the storage location

• Maintain information about access controls

• Maintain the link between preservation metadata and the record.

These capabilities are inherent in data grid technology and enforced for every digital object registered into the data grid. Policy58, rac-test-Immutability.r, demonstrates each of these capabilities.

Preservation also requires managing the properties of the archives while technology flows through the repository. This is accomplished by encapsulating the information needed to interact with a specific technology within a pluggable driver. For each new technology, a plug-in is created that supports interaction with the technology. Policies can be applied to control interactions with each plug-in.

A standard example is the use of a tape archive to hold records. A policy can be created that aggregates small files into a large tar file before the files are written to tape. Information about each small file is retained, while interactions with the tape drive are optimized.

An Archives Content Report, Archive-ARA, documents the holdings of an archive. It contains a list of all AIPs and their creation dates. The report is stored in GLOBAL_ACCOUNT/*Archive/GLOBAL_REPORTS.

Property Management:

- Policy77 – rac-listArchive.r

  ○ Generate a list of all of the AIPs in an archive and their creation dates. Store the list in Archive-ARA in the collection GLOBAL_ACCOUNT/*Archive/GLOBAL_REPORTS.

4.1.7   THE REPOSITORY SHALL PROVIDE THE PRODUCER/DEPOSITOR WITH APPROPRIATE RESPONSES AT AGREED POINTS DURING THE INGEST PROCESSES

Part of the submission agreement is the specification of the notifications that must be provided as records are ingested. Possible events that require notification are:

- Detection of an error in a SIP

- Formal acceptance of a SIP

- Change in an ingestion procedure

For the notification to be sent, an attribute needs to be created to define the e-mail address, Archive-Email, which is set on the GLOBAL_ACCOUNT/*Archive collection by Policy44, rac-setEmail.r.

The notifications are documented in the preservation action audit report, Archive-PAA. The SIP Ingestion Audit report, Archive-SIA, is derived from the Archive-PAA report through extraction of actions related to SIP ingestion. The Archive-PAA report is a manifest that is updated automatically with each notification and is included as part of the racNotify policy function.

Property Creation:

- Policy44 – rac-setEmail.r

  ○ Set the e-mail address to use when notifications are sent about events happening on an archives. The value of the Archive-Email attribute on the GLOBAL_ACCOUNT/*Archive collection is used for the e-mail address. The action is logged in Archive-PAA.

- Policy45 – rac-setAdminEmail.r

○ Set the repository administrator's e-mail address as the value for the attribute Repository-Email on the collection GLOBAL_ACCOUNT/GLOBAL_REPOSITORY. The action is logged in Archive-RAA.

Property Management:

• Policy46 – rac-notifyError.r

○ The generation of a notification event can be added to any policy. A policy function, racNotify, is provided that issues the notification to the required e-mail address. This function is added to Policy40, rac-verifySource.r, to send a notification when an error is detected. The example concatenates all errors into a single notification message. Note that messages are sent to every account that is defined by the Archive-Email attribute on the GLOBAL_ACCOUNT/*Archive collection. All notifications are logged in Archive-PAA, the Preservation Action Audit report, which is stored in GLOBAL_ACCOUNT/*Archive/GLOBAL_MANIFESTS.

Property Assessment:

• Policy47 – rac-verifyAttribute.r

○ Policy43, rac-verifyMetadata.r, is modified to send notification messages by adding a call to the policy function, racNotify. If missing attributes are detected, a message is sent to each person defined by the Archive-Email attribute on the collection that is being analyzed. Also a notification message is sent to the Repository administrator if the Archive-Email address is missing. The notification is logged in Archive-PAA, which is stored in GLOBAL_ACCOUNT/*Archive/GLOBAL_MANIFESTS.

4.1.8 THE REPOSITORY SHALL HAVE CONTEMPORANEOUS RECORDS OF ACTIONS AND ADMINISTRATION PROCESSES THAT ARE RELEVANT TO CONTENT ACQUISITION

Documentation of the actions and administrative processes relevant to content acquisition is required for audits. The actions that need to be recorded include:

• Confirmation receipts sent to providers

• Acquisition of preservation metadata for each record

• Actions taken while processing SIPs.

Relevant documents are:

Notifications of periodic review	Archive-NPRA	ISO 3.1.2.2
Content Information Deposition report	Archive-CIRA	ISO 4.1.1.2
Content Information Non-compliance report	Archive-CINCA	ISO 4.1.4
SIP compliance report	Archive-SIPCRA	ISO 4.1.5
Preservation Action Audit report	Archive-PAA	ISO 4.1.8

The Preservation Action Audit Report, Archive-PAA, logs all notifications sent to the SIP provider, including the e-mail address, the date, and the notification body. This is part of the racNotify (*Archive, *Msg) function. The document Archive-PAA is stored in GLOBAL_ACCOUNT/*Archive/GLOBAL_MANIFESTS and is managed by Policy3-Policy8, Policy26, Policy35, and Policy36.

4.2   INGEST: CREATION OF THE AIP

Documents that are used to manage creation of AIPs include:

AIP template for required metadata	Archive-AIP	ISO 4.2.1
Audit report of all actions	Archive-ARUA	ISO 4.2.10
SIP to AIP Process Description report	Archive-STAR	ISO 4.2.2
SIP Disposition Audit report	Archive-SAPA	ISO 4.2.3.1
Content Information Non-Compliance report	Archive-CINCA	ISO 4.2.7.3
AIP Compliance report	Archive-AIPCRA	ISO 4.2.8
Integrity report	Archive-INTA	ISO 4.2.9

4.2.1   THE REPOSITORY SHALL HAVE FOR EACH AIP OR CLASS OF AIPS PRESERVED BY THE REPOSITORY AN ASSOCIATED DEFINITION THAT IS ADEQUATE FOR PARSING THE AIP AND FIT FOR LONG-TERM PRESERVATION NEEDS

In the simplest form, an Archival Information Package consists of the original record plus information related to provenance, description, representation, intellectual property, access controls, and the Designated Community. These attributes can be considered unique to each record.

In addition to information about each individual record, information is also needed to identify relationships between records, such as arrangement in a series, information about the management of the records, such as chain of custody and preservation actions, and information about the use of the records, such as access logs. These attributes can be considered as being unique to an archives.

Both types of information can be captured as metadata attributes either associated with each AIP or associated with the collection holding the AIPs. An AIP template is externally generated to define the set of unique preservation information for each record.

This AIP template document, Archive-AIP, includes:

Archives – Packaging Information for the AIPs
Archives – Required provenance metadata attribute names
Archives – Required descriptive metadata attribute names
Archives – Required representation metadata attribute names
Archives – Required intellectual property ownership names
Archives – Required access control names
Archives – Required Designated Community ontology name

In this document, the Archive-AIP template is organized as a list of metadata attributes that are assigned to the collection GLOBAL_ARCHIVES. For each metadata attribute, an attribute name is defined, and an attribute value of RequiredAIP is set. An example is:

C-/lifelibZone/home/rwmoore/Archive-A/Archives |Audit-Depositor |RequiredAIP |
C-/lifelibZone/home/rwmoore/Archive-A/Archives |Audit-Source |RequiredAIP |

The AIP template is saved in the document Archive-AIP, and stored in GLOBAL_ACCOUNT/*Archive/GLOBAL_REPORTS. The AIP template is managed by Policy3-Policy8, Policy26, Policy35, and Policy36.

4.2.1.1 *The repository shall be able to identify which definition applies to which AIP.*

Information defining the name of the AIP template that will be used for records is registered as the attribute Archive-AIPTemplate on the collection GLOBAL_ACCOUNT/*Archive. This defines the name of the AIP template that is stored in GLOBAL_ACCOUNT/*Archive/GLOBAL_REPORTS. Policies are needed to load the AIP template, register the name, and verify that each AIP has the required metadata. The default name for the AIP template is Archive-AIP.

Property Creation:

- Policy48 – rac-setAIPTemplate.r

  ○ Set the name of the AIP template for records in *Archive using the meta-data attribute Archive-AIPTemplate and load the template into the collection

GLOBAL_ACCOUNT/*Archive/GLOBAL_REPORTS. This approach assumes that each *Archive holds records that can be processed using a single AIP template. The action is logged in Archive-PAA.

Property Assessment:

- Policy49 – rac-verifyAIPTemplate.r

    ○ Check that the attribute Archive-AIPTemplate has been set on each *Archive and verify that the referenced AIP template exists in the collection GLOBAL_ACCOUNT/*Archive/GLOBAL_REPORTS. The action is logged in GLOBAL_ACCOUNT/*Archive/GLOBAL_MANIFESTS/Archive-PAA.

4.2.1.2   *The repository shall have a definition of each AIP that is adequate for long-term preservation, enabling the identification and parsing of all the required components within that AIP.*

Each required component of an AIP is defined through a metadata attribute that is listed within the Archive-AIP template. Policy41, rac-setMetadata.r, provides the ability to parse the Archive-AIP template, extract the required metadata attributes, and add them to GLOBAL_ACCOUNT/*Archive/GLOBAL_ARCHIVES as required metadata.

Policy41 can be used to define required AIP attributes by adding lines to the Archive-META document specifying the GLOBAL_ARCHIVES collection and setting the attribute value to "RequiredAIP".

C-/lifelibZone/home/rwmoore/Archive-A/Archives |Audit-Depositor |RequiredAIP |
C-/lifelibZone/home/rwmoore/Archive-A/Archives |Audit-Source |RequiredAIP |

The required attributes for AIPs are loaded on the GLOBAL_ARCHIVES collection. The AIP attributes can be read from GLOBAL_ARCHIVES metadata and used to control the creation of AIP specific attributes. This has the advantage of allowing preservation metadata to be added incrementally, while still tracking the preservation requirements.

The inverse process is possible. The attributes can be extracted from the metadata catalog for a specific AIP and saved as a separate metadata file. This process is needed when generating Dissemination Information Packages, DIPS.

Property Creation:

- Policy50 – rac-createDIP.r

    ○ Create a metadata file that contains the metadata attributes associated with an AIP. The metadata file is named by adding "-meta" to the AIP name. The AIP metadata file is saved in a separate directory specified by

GLOBAL_ACCOUNT/*Archive/GLOBAL_DIPS. The action is logged in Archive-PAA.

4.2.2 THE REPOSITORY SHALL HAVE A DESCRIPTION OF HOW AIPS ARE CONSTRUCTED FROM SIPS

The report, Archive-STAR, documents the SIP to AIP processing steps. The report should contain the following information about the construction of an AIP from a SIP. Example steps would include:

- Identify the SIPS present in the GLOBAL_SIPS directory

- For each SIP, verify that the required attributes are present, that the record has the required format, and that the record has been processed to identify protected information, identify the presence of viruses, and verify compliance with the Designated Community ontology.

- Each SIP that passes the compliance test is assigned a compliance flag, Audit-Comply, with a value of "1".

- Periodically check the GLOBAL_SIPS collection for SIPS that have an Audit-Comply attribute with a value of "1", and copy the processed SIP into the GLOBAL_ARCHIVES directory.

- Generate an audit report, Archive-SAPA, documenting each successful generation of an AIP.

Values can be set for the Audit-Comply attribute to indicate the types of processing that were not completed successfully. Examples include setting Audit-Comply to:

- 0 indicating no processing has been done

- 1 indicating that all processing steps have been completed

- 2 indicating problems found by a virus-scan. The file must be deleted or modified. The Audit-CheckVirus flag is set to "1" if a virus is found and to "2" if there is no virus.

- 3 indicating presence of protected data. The file must be encrypted. The Audit-Check Protected flag is set to "1" when protected data is present and to "2" if the check passes.

- 4 indicating a disallowed data format. The file format must be converted. The Audit-CheckFormat flag is set to "1" for bad formats and to "2" for approved formats.

- 5 indicating that required metadata are missing. The metadata must be added. Note this analysis includes all types of required metadata. The Audit-CheckMetadata flag is set to "1" if metadata are missing and to "2" if required metadata are present.

- 6 indicating that metadata attribute values do not comply with the reserved vocabulary specified for the Designated Community. Additional attribute values are required that conform. The Audit-CheckVocab flag is set to "1" if unrecognized terms are used and to "2" for compliance with the reserved vocabulary list.

- 7 indicating that the file integrity was not preserved on receipt. The file must be replaced. The Audit-CheckIntegrity flag is set to "1" if the file is corrupted and to "2" if the integrity is good.

- 8 indicating that the record is a duplicate, modifying a previous record. A decision must be made whether a version is required. The Audit-CheckDup flag is set to "1" if the AIP already exists and to "2" if no AIP exists.

In each case, once a problem is corrected, all of the processing steps must be reapplied to ensure that the AIP is correctly formed from the SIP.

Additional processing flags may be needed to indicate restrictions that must be applied to the AIP after it is created. Examples include:

- Archive-Access restriction of access to identified accounts

- Archive-Distribution restriction of storage location to a specified system

- Archive-Replication specification of minimum number of required replicas

These processing steps do not affect the formation of the AIP, but do affect the management of the AIP.

The SIP to AIP processing steps document, Archive-STAR, is managed by Policy3-Policy8, Policy26, Policy35, and Policy36 and is stored in GLOBAL_ACCOUNT/*Archive/GLOBAL_REPORTS.

The formation of an AIP from a SIP is controlled by the following policies:

Property Creation:

- Policy51 – rac-checkSIP.r

    ○ Check the SIP for compliance with preservation requirements. Each type of check is encapsulated in a separate policy function. A processing flag stored on GLOBAL_ACCOUNT/*Archive/GLOBAL_SIPS controls whether a processing step should be done.

Check	Policy Function	Processing Flag
virus scan	racVirusCheck	Archive-CheckVirus
protected data	racProtectedDataCheck	Archive-CheckProtected
data format	racFormatCheck	Archive-CheckFormat
required metadata	racMetadataCheck	Archive-CheckMetadata
reserved vocabulary	racReservedVocabCheck	Archive-CheckVocab
integrity	racIntegrityCheck	Archive-CheckIntegrity
duplicates	racDupCheck	Archive-CheckDup

The compliance check invokes each Policy Function in turn for a specified SIP when the Processing Flag has the value "1". If all checks pass, the Audit-Comply flag is set to "1". The action is logged in Archive-PAA.

- Policy52 – rac-checkAllSIPS.r

  ○ Loop over all files in the GLOBAL_SIPS directory and evaluate type of error for all SIPs whose Audit-Comply flag is not equal to "1". Report all non-compliant SIPS in a version of the report Archive-SAPA, stored in the collection GLOBAL_ACCOUNT/*Archive/GLOBAL_REPORTS.

- Policy53 – rac-createAIP.r

  ○ Loop over all files in the GLOBAL_SIPS directory and copy compliant SIPS (Audit-Comply = "1") to the GLOBAL_ARCHIVES directory. Also set storage location, copy the metadata, set access controls, create the required replicas, and create a handle. A report Archive-AIPCRA is stored in GLOBAL_ACCOUNT/*Archive/GLOBAL_MANIFESTS that documents all problems.

Property Assessment:

- Policy54 – rac-checkAIP.r

  ○ Loop over all files in the GLOBAL_ARCHIVES directory and verify that each AIP has an Audit-Comply flag with a value of "1". Document results in the Archive-AIPCRA report, stored in GLOBAL_ACCOUNT/*Archive/GLOBAL_MANIFESTS.

4.2.3   THE REPOSITORY SHALL DOCUMENT THE FINAL DISPOSITION OF ALL SIPS

4.2.3.1 *The repository shall follow documented procedures if a SIP is not incorporated into an AIP or discarded and shall indicate why the SIP was not incorporated or discarded.*

The report, GLOBAL_ACCOUNT/*Archive/GLOBAL_REPORTS/Archive-SAPA, documents the status of all SIPS by parsing the Audit-Comply attribute. The SIPS in each category are identified. The report is generated by Policy52, rac-checkAllSIPS.r.

Each non-compliant report is listed. The number of non-compliant reports for the following categories is also listed. An example output is:

/lifelibZone/home/rwmoore/Archive-A/SIPS analyzed for compliance on 2016-07-19.15:57:23

> Totals for SIP compliance check
>> Virus check failed for 0 files
>> Protected data check failed for 0 files
>> Format check failed for 0 files
>> Metadata check failed for 0 files
>> Vocabulary check failed for 0 files
>> Integrity check failed for 0 files
>> Duplication check failed for 0 files

- Policy52 – rac-checkAllSIPS.r

  ○ Loop over all files in the GLOBAL_SIPS directory and evaluate type of error for all SIPs whose Audit-Comply flag is not equal to "1". Report all non-compliant SIPS in a version of the report Archive-SAPA, stored in the collection GLOBAL_ACCOUNT/*Archive/GLOBAL_REPORTS.

4.2.4   THE REPOSITORY SHALL HAVE AND USE A CONVENTION THAT GENERATES PERSISTENT, UNIQUE IDENTIFIERS FOR ALL AIPS

The identifiers assigned to AIPs are chosen to support specific operations. The identifiers that may be used include:

Type of Identifier	Source of Identifier	Identifier Implementation
Globally unique ID	Handle system	Repository-Handle
Location	Handle system	Repository-Handle

Access control	iRODS ticket	URL
Arrangement	iRODS logical name	Data grid name
Description	iRODS AVU	Data grid metadata
Internal unique ID	iRODS state	DATA_ID

In the AIP generation process, Policy53 – rac-createAIP.r, creates a handle when the Process Flag, Archive-CheckHandle" has a value of "1". The flag is retrieved from the collection GLOBAL_ACCOUNT/*Archive/GLOBAL_ARCHIVES.

Property Creation:

• Policy53 – rac-createAIP.r

  ○ Loop over all files in the GLOBAL_SIPS directory and copy compliant SIPS (Audit-Comply = "1") to the GLOBAL_ARCHIVES directory. Also set storage location, copy the metadata, set access controls, create the required replicas, and create a handle. Store results in Archive-AIPCRA in the collection GLOBAL_ACCOUNT/*Archive/GLOBAL_MANIFESTS.

Property Management:

• Policy56 – rac-createHandle.r

  ○ Set a handle for a specific file in GLOBAL_ACCOUNT/*Archive/GLOBAL_ARCHIVES. This may need to be used if the handle for a file is corrupted and a new handle is required. Log action in Archive-PAA.

Property Assessment:

• Policy57 – rac-checkHandle.r

  ○ Check that a handle exists for each AIP in GLOBAL_ACCOUNT/*Archive/GLOBAL_ARCHIVES. Log action in Archive-PAA.

4.2.4.1 *The repository shall uniquely identify each AIP within the repository.*

Each AIP is assigned identifiers by the data grid when the file is loaded into the repository.

Identifier TYPE	Identifier Name
iRODS internal identifier	DATA_ID
iRODS logical name	ZONE_NAME/DATA_COLL_NAME/DATA_NAME

Storage name	DATA_RESC_NAME
Storage path on storage system	DATA_PATH
Replica number	DATA_REPL_NUM
Checksum	DATA_CHECKSUM

A globally unique identifier can be assigned using the Handle system. Within the data grid, an external service can be invoked to assign a Handle. This capability is encapsulated in the policy function racCreateHandle, and is invoked by the policies rac-createAIP.r and rac-createHandle.r.

Property Creation:

- Policy53 – rac-createAIP.r

  ○ Loop over all files in the GLOBAL_SIPS directory and copy compliant SIPS (Audit-Comply = "1") to the GLOBAL_ARCHIVES directory. Also set storage location, copy the metadata, set access controls, create the required replicas, and create a handle. The handle is stored as the metadata attribute Audit-Handle. The process results are stored in Archive-AIPCRA.

- Policy56 – rac-createHandle.r

  ○ Set a handle for a specific file in GLOBAL_ACCOUNT/*Archive/GLOBAL_ARCHIVES. This may need to be used if the handle for a file is corrupted and a new handle is required. The handle is stored as the metadata attribute Audit-Handle. The action is logged in Archive-PAA.

4.2.4.1.1   The repository shall have unique identifiers.

Each AIP is assigned multiple identifiers, which are all unique:

1. Logical name, consisting of ZONE_NAME/COLL_NAME/DATA_NAME

2. Storage name, consisting of DATA_RESC_NAME/DATA_PATH

3. Internal data grid identifier, consisting of ZONE_NAME/DATA_ID

4. Handle, stored in Audit-Handle attribute on the file.

4.2.4.1.2   The repository shall assign and maintain persistent identifiers of the AIP and its components so as to be unique within the context of the repository.

The creation of persistent identifiers assumes that the identifiers are assigned to immutable digital objects. Within an iRODS data grid, digital objects can be migrated to alternate storage locations, and replicas can be created and deleted. In both cases, the persistent identifiers should not change. Policy58, rac-testImmutability.r, tests whether digital object identifiers, checksum values, and metadata assigned to a digital object remain invariant under data movement operations applied within the data grid. The operations include replication, deletion of a replica, and physical movement of a file to another storage system. An example of the output from Policy58, rac-testImmutability.r, is listed below. The results are written to Archive-RAA.

Testing immutability of persistent file names on 2016-08-17.14:24:29

For initial
    /lifelibZone/home/rwmoore/tRFile, DATA_ID = 1129171, DATA_COLL_ID = 21854
    /lifelibZone/home/rwmoore/tRFile,   DATA_CHECKSUM   =   sha2:Y+qZuU8GCRQtw44x/XOQQ02/
    mk+sElDmPG4Lwg0LMG0=
    /lifelibZone/home/rwmoore/tRFile, DATA_REPL_NUM = 0, DATA_RESC_NAME = LTLResc
    /lifelibZone/home/rwmoore/tRFile, DATA_PATH = /fs1/lifelibVault/home/rwmoore/tRFile
    /lifelibZone/home/rwmoore/tRFile, DATA_ID = 1129171, DATA_COLL_ID = 21854
    /lifelibZone/home/rwmoore/tRFile,   DATA_CHECKSUM   =   sha2:Y+qZuU8GCRQtw44x/XOQQ02/
    mk+sElDmPG4Lwg0LMG0=
    /lifelibZone/home/rwmoore/tRFile, DATA_REPL_NUM = 1, DATA_RESC_NAME = LTLResc
    /lifelibZone/home/rwmoore/tRFile,   DATA_PATH   =   /snprojects/iren2/lifetimelib/renci-unix1/Vault/home/
    rwmoore/tRFile
    /lifelibZone/home/rwmoore/tRFile, Audit-Handle = 123456789
After replica delete
    /lifelibZone/home/rwmoore/tRFile, DATA_ID = 1129171, DATA_COLL_ID = 21854
    /lifelibZone/home/rwmoore/tRFile,   DATA_CHECKSUM   =   sha2:Y+qZuU8GCRQtw44x/XOQQ02/
    mk+sElDmPG4Lwg0LMG0=
    /lifelibZone/home/rwmoore/tRFile, DATA_REPL_NUM = 0, DATA_RESC_NAME = LTLResc
    /lifelibZone/home/rwmoore/tRFile, DATA_PATH = /fs1/lifelibVault/home/rwmoore/tRFile
    /lifelibZone/home/rwmoore/tRFile, Audit-Handle = 123456789
After replica create
     /lifelibZone/home/rwmoore/tRFile, DATA_ID = 1129171, DATA_COLL_ID = 21854
    /lifelibZone/home/rwmoore/tRFile,   DATA_CHECKSUM   =   sha2:Y+qZuU8GCRQtw44x/XOQQ02/
    mk+sElDmPG4Lwg0LMG0=
    /lifelibZone/home/rwmoore/tRFile, DATA_REPL_NUM = 0, DATA_RESC_NAME = LTLResc
    /lifelibZone/home/rwmoore/tRFile, DATA_PATH = /fs1/lifelibVault/home/rwmoore/tRFile
    /lifelibZone/home/rwmoore/tRFile, Audit-Handle - 123456789
After file migrated
    /lifelibZone/home/rwmoore/tRFile, DATA_ID = 1129171, DATA_COLL_ID = 21854
    /lifelibZone/home/rwmoore/tRFile,   DATA_CHECKSUM   =   sha2:Y+qZuU8GCRQtw44x/XOQQ02/
    mk+sElDmPG4Lwg0LMG0=
    /lifelibZone/home/rwmoore/tRFile, DATA_REPL_NUM = 0, DATA_RESC_NAME = demoResc

/lifelibZone/home/rwmoore/tRFile, DATA_PATH = /var/lib/irods/iRODS/demoResc/Vault/home/rwmoore/
tRFile
/lifelibZone/home/rwmoore/tRFile, Audit-Handle = 123456789

Note that the DATA_NAME, DATA_ID, and DATA_COLL_ID do not change. The DATA_CHECKSUM does not change, and the Audit-Handle does not change. Note that the DATA_CHECKSUM is generated using SHA-256 encoding. The storage location and number of replicas do change as a result of the operations that are applied.

Property Assessment:

- Policy58 – rac-testImmutability.r

    ○ Create a test file and verify that when persistent identifiers are assigned to a file, the linkages are preserved as files are migrated between storage systems and replicas are created and deleted. This means that
    DATA_NAME, DATA_COLL_ID, DATA_ID, DATA_CHECKSUM, and Audit-Handle should remain fixed. The result is logged in Archive-RAA.

4.2.4.1.3   Documentation shall describe any processes used for changes to such identifiers.

The procedures for changing persistent identifiers is part of the Standard Operating Procedure, Archive-SOP, defined in ISO 3.5.1.2.

Changes to persistent identifiers may occur under the following situations:

- If an AIP is overwritten, the DATA_CHECKSUM will change. This is protected by Policy53, rac-createAIP.r, which verifies whether an AIP exists before creating a new AIP. If the AIP is already present, an error notification is sent to the GLOBAL_EMAIL.

- If an AIP is copied to a new logical name, the DATA_ID, DATA_COLL_ID, and DATA_NAME will change. The Audit-Handle will be deleted, and a new handle will need to be created with Policy56, rac-createHandle.r.

- If an AIP is deleted, the Audit-Handle attribute is unlinked from the AIP.

4.2.4.1.4   The repository shall be able to provide a complete list of all such identifiers and do spot checks for duplications.

A query can be issued to check whether duplicate identifiers exist. The data grid creates a unique DATA_ID identifier each time a file is loaded into the system. Note that the same DATA_NAME may occur in different collections (different DATA_COLL_ID values). However, if an attempt is made to add a DATA_NAME to a collection where the DATA_NAME already exists, an error message is generated. It is possible to force an overwrite of the new file on top of the old file, changing the DATA_CHECKSUM.

When metadata attributes are added to a file, a check is made to determine whether the META_DATA_ATTR_NAME and META_DATA_ATTR_VALUE are already present on the file. If the name and value already exist, the operation is not executed. It is possible to have the same attribute name appear multiple times, but each time the associated attribute value must be different. This makes it possible to associate multiple Archive-Email addresses with an *Archive.

The values for Audit-Handle can be checked for duplicates, along with the DATA_NAME and DATA_COLL_ID of the collisions.

Property Assessment:

- Policy59 – rac-CheckDuplicates.r

  ○ List all values of Audit-Handle in a sorted list. Identify all duplicates and list the file names. A report is generated in GLOBAL_ACCOUNT/*Archive/GLOBAL_REPORTS/Archive-IDCA.

4.2.4.1.5   The system of identifiers shall be adequate to fit the repository's current and foreseeable future requirements such as numbers of objects.

The identifiers used by the data grid, DATA_ID, DATA_NAME, DATA_COLL_ID, DATA_CHECKSUM scale to the billions of files. The identifier created by the Handle system can also scale to a very large number of files.

Existing production systems have hundreds of millions of files, and hundreds of millions of attributes.

4.2.4.2   The repository shall have a system of reliable linking/resolution services in order to find the uniquely identified object, regardless of its physical location.

The linking of identifiers to names is illustrated by Policy58, rac-testImmutability.r. As a file is physically moved between locations, the persistent identifiers remain unchanged. The data grid automatically updates the DATA_PATH and DATA_RESC_NAME to point to the new storage locations.

The technology used to manage the state information is a relational database.

4.2.5   THE REPOSITORY SHALL HAVE ACCESS TO NECESSARY TOOLS AND RESOURCES TO PROVIDE AUTHORITATIVE REPRESENTATION INFORMATION FOR ALL OF THE DIGITAL OBJECTS IT CONTAINS

Representation information includes the file type or format. A normal concern is that a file format can become obsolete, and may no longer be parsable.

A concept of persistent objects can be implemented, in which the AIP format is never changed. Instead, parsing mechanisms are maintained that enable the interpretation and display of records using the original parser. The parsers are encapsulated in Docker containers (a form of virtual machine environment) that enable the parsers to be run at any site that has a Docker Engine.

A project which uses this approach is iBiblio, http://www.ibiblio.org. A second project is Cyverse, http://www.cyverse.org, which provides the Discovery Environment for encapsulating applications in Docker containers. As new data formats are added to the repository, associated tools for parsing the formats can be added.

If modern display mechanisms are required, a transformative migration of an AIP format can be done. An example of a service that supports format migration is the Brown Dog Data Infrastructure Building Block (DIBBS) project. The Brown Dog service can also be encapsulated in a Docker container and applied at the storage location of each AIP.

4.2.5.1   *The repository shall have tools or methods to identify the file type of all submitted Data Objects.*

The file type of an AIP can be determined multiple ways:

- Through extraction of the extension associated with the AIP file name

- As an explicit attribute that is loaded at the same time as the AIP

- Through an external service that parses the AIP for magic numbers that are unique to a specific file type. An example is the DROID file format identification services supported by the National Archives and available at http://www.nationalarchives.gov. uk/information-management/manage-information/preserving-digital-records/droid. The service can be downloaded and encapsulated in a Docker container. The file types are stored in the PRONOM technical registry, http://apps.nationalarchives.gov.uk/ PRONOM/Default.aspx.

Policies can be written to access a desired service for identifying a file format.

Property Creation:

- Policy60 – rac-setFormat.r

○ Set the file type in the state information, DATA_TYPE_NAME, based on the file extension. The action is logged in Archive-PAA.

4.2.5.2 *The repository shall have tools or methods to determine what Representation Information is necessary to make each Data Object understandable to the Designated Community.*

The required Representation Information depends upon the choice of services for parsing the data format. The approach that we take is to use the concept of Persistent Objects, in which the original format of the Digital Object is maintained, along with a parsing application that is encapsulated in a machine image. We use the Docker container system to eliminate effort associated with porting the Docker containers to different operating systems.

The Brown Dog format transformation services are used to parse and display each data format. The Brown Dog services are encapsulated in a Docker container, managed through the Discovery Environment, and executed under the control of policies within the iRODS data grid.

Property Management:

• Policy61 – rac-invokeService.r

○ Defines a standard mechanism for invoking an external asynchronous service. Note that the response may be recorded as metadata assigned to the AIP, and the transformed file may be directly deposited into the data grid. The action is logged in Archive-PAA.

4.2.5.3 *The repository shall have access to the requisite Representation Information.*

The representation information is stored as metadata attributes associated with each AIP. The required information includes the format type and the access controls.

DATA_TYPE_NAME   File format type

Property Management:

• Policy50 – rac-createDIP.r

○ The metadata attributes for an AIP are recorded in a metadata file. The metadata file is named by adding "-meta" to the AIP name. The AIP metadata file is saved in a separate directory specified by GLOBAL_ACCOUNT/*Archive/GLOBAL_DIPS. The action is logged in Archive-PAA.

4.2.5.4 *The repository shall have tools or methods to ensure that the requisite Representation Information is persistently associated with the relevant Data Objects.*

The metadata attributes for an AIP are directly linked through the iCAT catalog with the file that contains the AIP content. For each file the following schema indirection is used:

iRODS State Information	Definition
META_DATA_ATTR_NAME	Lists the name of the metadata attribute
META_DATA_ATTR_VALUE	Lists the value of the metadata attribute
META_DATA_ATTR_UNITS	Lists a comment field
META_DATA_ATTR_ID	Assigns a unique identifier
META_DATA_ATTR_CREATE_TIME	Assigns the creation time
META_DATA_ATTR_MODIFY_TIME	Assigns a modification time

Multiple types of database technology can be used to hold the iCAT catalog. In iRODS version 4.3, the choices are extended through the QueryArrow interface. QueryArrow virtualizes metadata. The system manages the properties of the metadata independently of the choice of database technology. Properties can include:

- Access controls

- Auditing

- Distribution

- Federation

- Migration

- Retention

The types of databases that can be used include:

- Relational database (Oracle, Postgresql, Mysql, SQLite)

- Graph database (Neo4j)

- ElasticSearch index

- In-memory data structures

4.2.6 THE REPOSITORY SHALL HAVE DOCUMENTED PROCESSES FOR ACQUIRING PRESERVATION DESCRIPTION INFORMATION (PDI) FOR ITS ASSOCIATED CONTENT INFORMATION AND ACQUIRE PDI IN ACCORDANCE WITH THE DOCUMENTED PROCESSES

Preservation Description information defines how an AIP will be managed and provides an auditable trail for validating claims of authenticity. The description of the source is done through the metadata attributes Audit-Source and Audit-Depositor. The description of the content is provided through description metadata, Audit-Description. To guarantee authenticity, information is also needed that tracks all operations performed upon the AIP within the repository. An audit trail of all actions applied to the processing of a SIP and management of an AIP is needed to detect changes to the digital holdings.

The management attributes include:

Audit-Access	Access restrictions required for an AIP
Audit-Depositor	Depositor of a SIP that is formatted into an AIP
Audit-Distribution	Required storage locations for the AIP
Audit-Source	Source of a SIP that is formatted into an AIP

The audit reports that are used to track actions applied to the digital objects include:

Content Information Non-Compliance report	Archive-CINCA	ISO 4.1.4
Preservation Action Audit report	Archive-PAA	ISO 4.1.8
Audit report of all actions	Archive-ARUA	ISO 4.2.10
SIP Disposition Audit report	Archive-SAPA	ISO 4.2.3.1
Handle Duplicate Audit report	Archive-IDCA	ISO 4.2.4.1.4
AIP Compliance report	Archive-AIPCRA	ISO 4.2.8
Integrity report	Archive-INTA	ISO 4.2.9
Access log	Archive-ALA	ISO 4.6.1
Error reports	Archive-ERR	ISO 4.6.2.1

The Archive-ARUA report is generated from an audit trail of all actions applied in the repository, and is the ultimate source for tracking actions.

4.2.6.1 *The repository shall have documented processes for acquiring PDI.*

For each of the listed reports, a policy either documents an action as it is applied within the repository, or extracts information from the metadata managed by the repository. Two policy functions are essential for automating the tracking of actions:

racSaveFile (*File, *Rep) – save the contents of stdout to *File in the GLOBAL_ACCOUNT/*Rep/GLOBAL_REPORTS collection and create a version of the file in the GLOBAL_ACCOUNT/*Rep/GLOBAL_VERSIONS collection. This function is called every time a report is generated. The function:

- Checks which collection should hold the report, GLOBAL_REPOSITORY or *Archive

- Creates GLOBAL_REPORTS directory if needed

- Creates GLOBAL_VERSIONS directory if needed

- Copies stdout to *File

- Stores *File in GLOBAL_REPORTS

- Checksums the file *File

- Replicates the file *File

- Versions the file *File, storing a version in the GLOBAL_VERSIONS collection

- Sets a default Repository-Report attribute on the collection GLOBAL_REPOSITORY or Archive-Report attribute on the collection *Archive if the attribute is missing

- Sets an Audit-Date attribute for when the report should be updated

- Verifies the checksum of the versioned file

- Replicates the versioned file

- Verifies the checksum of the replicated file

racWriteManifest (*OutFile, *Rep, *Source) – append the contents of *Source to the file *OutFile in the collection GLOBAL_ACCOUNT/*Rep/GLOBAL_MANIFESTS. This function is called every time a manifest file is updated. The function:

- Creates GLOBAL_ACCOUNT/*Rep/GLOBAL_MANIFESTS directories if needed

- Creates the manifest file, *OutFile, if needed in the collection GLOBAL_ACCOUNT/*Rep/GLOBAL_MANIFESTS

- Appends the information in *Source to the end of *OutFile

- Resets the checksum of the manifest file

- Updates the replica of the manifest file

- Verifies the checksum of the replica of the versioned file

A policy can either directly update metadata in the iCAT catalog, or record information in a versioned report (racSaveFile) or add logging information to a manifest file (racWriteManifest). For each ISO policy, the auditing mechanism is identified.

4.2.6.2 *The repository shall execute its documented processes for acquiring PDI.*

Policy-based systems automate the enforcement of management policies through use of a rule engine. Each time a policy is executed, the racSaveFile and racWriteManifest policy functions can be automatically executed. This produces explicitly named files that document preservation actions.

The iRODS data grid version 4.2 also automates application of auditing rules. A meta-rule is defined that is applied at each policy-enforcement point. This permits tracking of all operations performed within the repository at the level of interactions with files, metadata, and users. A single action such as the loading of a SIP can invoke the recording of information from more than 150 policy enforcement points, tracking interactions with user clients and archive technology.

Property Creation:

- Policy62 – rac-auditRule.re

  ○ This example audit policy is automatically applied at each policy enforcement point to record the outcome of an operation and the controlling parameters. Depending upon the collection, different actions can be logged. The results are indexed in ElasticSearch.

4.2.6.3 *The repository shall ensure that the PDI is persistently associated with the relevant Content Information.*

The external index created by the auditing rule lists the persistent state information for the objects on which the actions have been applied. This state information includes:

Type of Attribute	Value of Attribute
DATA_NAME	Name of the digital object
DATA_COLL_ID	Identifier of the collection holding the object
$userNameClient	Identifier of the person applying the action
*Time	Time stamp for when the action occurred

The combination of DATA_NAME and DATA_COLL_ID defines a unique identifier for the digital object within the data grid. A unique internal identifier is also created, DATA_ID. A query can be made on DATA_ID to identify all state information and metadata associated with the digital object.

4.2.7 THE REPOSITORY SHALL ENSURE THAT THE CONTENT INFORMATION OF THE AIPS IS UNDERSTANDABLE FOR THEIR DESIGNATED COMMUNITY AT THE TIME OF CREATION OF THE AIP

A context is required for each Data Object for the Designated Community to understand the meaning and relevance of each SIP. The context is captured in metadata attributes registered for each AIP:

Audit-Description	Descriptive metadata defining the context
Audit-Ontology	Name of the knowledge base for validating the context

4.2.7.1   Repository shall have a documented process for testing understandability for their Designated Communities of the Content Information of the AIPs at their creation.

The description information is explicitly loaded with each SIP as metadata attributes specified within an Archive-META file. Each line of the Archive-META file defines a SIP name, the associated descriptive attribute name, "Audit-Description", the descriptive attribute value, and a descriptive attribute comment. Policy42, rac-inputMetadata.r, is used to load the information:

Property Creation:

- Policy42- rac-inputMetadata.r

    ○ Read pipe-delimited metadata files and load the attributes onto a SIP. A standard name for the metadata file is the record name with "-meta" appended. The actions are logged to Archive-SIPCRA. The format of the file is

    /lifelibZone/home/rwmoore/Archive-A/SIPS/rec3 |Audit-Description |First line |
    /lifelibZone/home/rwmoore/Archive-A/SIPS/rec3 |Audit-Description | Second line |

As many lines of description as needed can be assigned to a SIP. When the AIP is created, the metadata attributes from the SIP are copied onto the AIP.

The description of the content Information should comply with an ontology that defines the Designated Community. The tool used to validate the description against the Audit-Ontology is the Helping Interdisciplinary Vocabulary Engineering (HIVE) service. This is an external service that can be encapsulated within a Docker container and applied locally within the repository. The Docker container is managed by the Discovery Environment, which links files in the iRODS data grid to workflows that access services encapsulated in Docker containers. A policy function that invokes the HIVE service is

- **racReservedVocabCheck (*File, *Coll, *Archive, *S6)** – Check whether a SIP uses approved vocabulary for descriptive metadata.

The Archive-HVOA report lists the ontology that is associated with an *Archive. The report is stored in
GLOBAL_ACCOUNT/*Archive/GLOBAL_REPORTS.

Property Management:

- Policy78 – rac-listVocab.r

   ○ Access the HIVE system to retrieve a copy of the reserved vocabulary that is used to validate descriptive metadata, and store the list in the document Archive-HVOA.

4.2.7.2 *The repository shall execute the testing process for each class of Content Information of the AIPs.*

When an AIP is generated from a SIP, Policy51, rac-checkSIP.r, applies all required processing steps. This includes applying the racReservedVocabCheck. Note that a process control flag determines whether or not to check the reserved vocabulary. If the Audit-CheckVocab attribute on the GLOBAL_ACCOUNT/*Archive/GLOBAL_SIPS collection has the value of "1", the check is performed. Otherwise the test is skipped. The vocabulary to use for verification is defined by the attribute Archive-Ontology, which is set on the
GLOBAL_ACCOUNT/*Archive/GLOBAL_ARCHIVES collection.

Property Assessment:

- Policy51 – rac-checkSIP.r

   ○ Checks a SIP for compliance with preservation policies. The policy function racCheckMetadata is invoked to verify the terms used within Audit-Description are consistent with terms listed in the knowledge ontology. The action is logged in Archive-PAA.

4.2.7.3 *The repository shall bring the Content Information of the AIP up to the required level of understandability if it fails the understandability testing.*

The required level of understandability is determined by the Designated Community. The reserved vocabulary ontology is a proxy for the Designated Community that can be accessed dynamically.

Each term used in the description can be checked against the knowledge ontology. If a problem is found with the descriptive terms, the attribute Audit-CheckVocab is set to "1" on the SIP. All AIPs inherit the SIP attributes when they are created. Normally, if the vocabulary check is not passed, the AIP creation is not done. However, a process control flag, Archive-CheckVocab, can be set on GLOBAL_ACCOUNT/*Archive/GLOBAL_SIPS to a value of "0" to skip the check. An implication is the need for a policy to verify the AIPS for compliance with a vocabulary check.

Property Management:

- Policy63 – rac-checkVocab.r

  ○ A check is made on all AIPs to identify digital records that need additional processing. A notification message is sent to the archive administrator when problems are found. The results are stored in Archive-CINCA.

4.2.8   THE REPOSITORY SHALL VERIFY EACH AIP FOR COMPLETENESS AND CORRECTNESS AT THE POINT IT IS CREATED

Two sets of preservation policies must be applied when AIPs are created from SIPs. The required provenance metadata, representation metadata, and description metadata must be present on the SIP. In addition, the AIP must also satisfy policies related to AIP management such as access controls, replication, and distribution.

These checks are implemented by Policy51, rac-checkSIP.r, and Policy53, rac-createAIP.r. Each SIP is checked for compliance with required metadata in Policy51. If the SIP passes the check, the flag Audit-Comply is set to "1". In Policy53, a check is made that the Audit-Comply flag has been set, and policies for access, replication, and distribution are applied. A report is generated documenting all problems in GLOBAL_ACCOUNT/*Archive/GLOBAL_MANIFESTS/Archive-AIPCRA. Checks for compliance are also needed after non-compliant SIPs are corrected. Policy54, rac-checkAIP.r, checks all AIPs for compliance based on the value of the Audit-Comply flag.

Property Creation:

- Policy53 – rac-createAIP.r

  ○ Loop over all files in the GLOBAL_SIPS directory and copy compliant SIPS (Audit-Comply = "1") to the GLOBAL_ARCHIVES directory. Also set storage location, copy the metadata, set access controls, create the required replicas, and create a handle. A report Archive-AIPCRA is stored in GLOBAL_ACCOUNT/*Archive/GLOBAL_MANIFESTS that documents all problems.

Property Assessment:

- Policy51 – rac-checkSIP.r

  ○ Checks a SIP for compliance with preservation policies. The policy function racCheckMetadata is invoked to verify the terms used within Audit-Description are consistent with terms listed in the knowledge ontology. The action is logged in Archive-PAA.

- Policy54 – rac-checkAIP.r

  ○ Loop over all files in the GLOBAL_ARCHIVES directory and verify that each AIP has an Audit-Comply flag with a value of "1". Document results in the Archive-AIPCRA report, stored in GLOBAL_ACCOUNT/*Archive/GLOBAL_MANIFESTS.

4.2.9   THE REPOSITORY SHALL PROVIDE AN INDEPENDENT MECHANISM FOR VERIFYING THE INTEGRITY OF THE REPOSITORY COLLECTION/CONTENT

The integrity of the repository needs to be verified independently of the mechanisms provided by the storage systems. A standard approach is to calculate a checksum for each digital object, and compare the value with a saved value of the checksum that was generated when the digital object was created.

Each digital object has a persistent state information attribute called DATA_CHECKSUM. This is the original value of the checksum for the digital object. Every digital object can be read, a new value for the checksum can be calculated, and the new value can be compared with the saved value. A report is generated that documents all corrupted files that are found.

Property Assessment:

- Policy29 – rac-verifyIntegrity.r

  ○ Verify the checksum of each file in all of the *Archive collections and replace bad files with a good replica.

  ○ Note that each of the separate archive collections are checked. A periodic rule is initiated to do the checks yearly. Results are written to GLOBAL_ACCOUNT/GLOBAL_REPOSITORY/GLOBAL_MANIFESTS/Archive-RCA

- Policy64 – rac-verifyIntegrityArchive.r

  ○ Verify the checksum of each file in a specific *Archive collection.

     ◦ The rule is run interactively. Results are written to
GLOBAL_ACCOUNT/*Archive/GLOBAL_MANIFESTS/Archive-INTA.

4.2.10 THE REPOSITORY SHALL HAVE CONTEMPORANEOUS RECORDS OF ACTIONS AND ADMINISTRATION PROCESSES THAT ARE RELEVANT TO AIP CREATION

The documents that track all actions and administration processes relevant to AIP creation are:

Content Information Non-Compliance report	Archive-CINCA	ISO 4.1.4
Preservation Action Audit report	Archive-PAA	ISO 4.1.8
Audit Report of all actions	Archive-ARUA	ISO 4.2.10
SIP Disposition Audit report	Archive-SAPA	ISO 4.2.3.1
Handle Duplicate Audit report	Archive-IDCA	ISO 4.2.4.1.4
AIP Compliance report	Archive-AIPCRA	ISO 4.2.8
Integrity report	Archive-INTA	ISO 4.2.9
Access log	Archive-ALA	ISO 4.6.1
Error reports	Archive-ERR	ISO 4.6.2.1

The document that tracks all operations performed for preservation is Archive-PAA, which is stored in GLOBAL_ACCOUNT/*Archive/GLOBAL_MANIFESTS. The tracking is done through explicit calls to racWriteManifest within the preservation policies. The report Audit-AURA is generated by parsing the audit trail to identify all operations performed upon files in an *Archive collection. The audit trail is indexed in ElasticSearch. The Audit-AURA report is created by querying ElasticSearch through the Discovery Environment.

Property Creation:

- Policy62 – rac-auditRule.re

  ◦ The example audit policy is automatically applied at each policy enforcement point to record the outcome of an operation and the controlling parameters. Depending upon the collection, different actions can be logged.

Property Assessment:

- Policy65 – rac-createAudit.r

  ◦ The example audit report generation policy queries the ElasticSearch index for events that modify files in GLOBAL_ACCOUNT/*Archive. The results are saved in GLOBAL_ACCOUNT/*Archive/GLOBAL_REPORTS/Archive-ARUA.

4.3   PRESERVATION PLANNING

Documents that support preservation planning include:

Preservation Strategic Plan	Archive-PSP	ISO 3.1.2
Preservation Policies	Archive-PPA	ISO 3.3.2
Preservation Implementation Plan	Archive-PIP	ISO 3.3.2.1
Designated Community Review	Archive-DCR	ISO 4.3.2
HIVE Vocabulary Ontology	Archive-HVOA	ISO 4.3.2.1
Docker Image Report	Archive-DIRA	ISO 4.3.3.1

4.3.1   THE REPOSITORY SHALL HAVE DOCUMENTED PRESERVATION STRATEGIES RELEVANT TO ITS HOLDINGS

The preservation strategy relies upon computer actionable rules to enforce:

- Authenticity

- Integrity

- Chain of Custody

- Original arrangement

Authenticity is maintained by linking provenance information to each AIP (Audit-Source, Audit-Depositor) using Policy39, rac-setSource.r. Integrity is maintained by replicating the files and saving a checksum (Policy26, rac-setChecksum.re), and periodically verifying integrity (Policy 29, rac-verifyIntegrity.r). Chain of Custody is maintained by managing access controls (Policy31, rac-setAccess.r), and tracking actions performed upon the AIPs (Policy65, rac-createAudit.r). The original arrangement is maintained through the creation of collections that mimic the original order of records in a series. Note that the *Archive collection can have sub-collections that will be automatically controlled by policies that use recursion on collection names.

4.3.2   THE REPOSITORY SHALL HAVE MECHANISMS IN PLACE FOR MONITORING ITS PRESERVATION ENVIRONMENT

The preservation environment needs to be monitored to ensure that all of the systems are operational. An administration interface tracks the status of each storage system, the status of the database, the status of the data grid servers, the status of the external services, the status of the network, and the status of the authentication systems.

The repository configuration is retrieved using a Unix shell command, izonereport. The administrative tool izonereport queries the entire iRODS Zone for configuration information. The configuration information is generated in the form of a JSON document which can be validated using schemas found at https://schemas.irods.org. This ensures that the data grid is configured correctly.

An example of an administration interface is the belphegor interface to the Discovery Environment. This verifies that all system components are running.

4.3.2.1 *The repository shall have mechanisms in place for monitoring and notification when Representation Information is inadequate for the Designated Community to understand the data holdings.*

The Designated Community is able to understand the data holdings when the data formats comply with expected standards. The Designated Community can be queried periodically to determine if their requirements have changed. The actions are documented in an externally generated report called Archive-DCR, Designated Community Review. The document is stored in GLOBAL_ACCOUNT/*Archive/GLOBAL_REPORTS/Archive-DCR, and is managed by Policy3-Policy8, Policy26, Policy35, and Policy36. The document contains:

Archives – Surveys of the Designated Community
Operations – Documentation of processes for monitoring the preservation environment

The desired data formats are defined by the preservation attribute
  Archive-Format.
The attribute is defined on the collections
GLOBAL_ACCOUNT/*Archive/GLOBAL_ARCHIVES & GLOBAL_SIPS.
  Property Creation:
  • Policy41 – rac-setMetadata.r

    ◦ Read a pipe-delimited metadata file and set the required SIP metadata attributes on a specified collection name. The format of the file is

      C-/lifelibZone/home/rwmoore/Archive-A/SIPS |Audit-Depositor |RequiredSIP |
      C-/lifelibZone/home/rwmoore/Archive-A/SIPS |Audit-Source |RequiredSIP |
      C-/lifelibZone/home/rwmoore/Archive-A/SIPS |Archive-Format |RequiredSIP |
      C-/lifelibZone/home/rwmoore/Archive-A/SIPS |Archive-IPR |RequiredSIP |
      C-/lifelibZone/home/rwmoore/Archive-A/SIPS |Archive-Ontology |RequiredSIP |
      C-/lifelibZone/home/rwmoore/Archive-A/SIPS |Archive-Description |RequiredSIP |

    The action is logged in Archive-PAA.

  • Policy60 – rac-setFormat.r

    ◦ Extract the file type based on the file extension and set the file type in the state information, DATA_TYPE_NAME. The action is logged in Archive-PAA.

Property Management:

- Policy38 – rac-surveyArchive.r

  ○ Analyze GLOBAL_ACCOUNT/*Archive/GLOBAL_ARCHIVES to survey the contents. Generate metrics for size, number of files, types of files, and most recent deposition. The report, Archive-CIRA, is stored in GLOBAL_ACCOUNT/*Archive/GLOBAL_REPORTS

Property Assessment:

- Policy66 – rac-checkFormat.r

  ○ Check that the format on each AIP corresponds to a format specified by Archive-Format. The required format is defined in Archive-DCR, Designated Community. The results of the check are written to Archive-PAA.

4.3.3 THE REPOSITORY SHALL HAVE MECHANISMS TO CHANGE ITS PRESERVATION PLANS AS A RESULT OF ITS MONITORING ACTIVITIES

The preservation plans may change through the addition of new requirements for representation information, or descriptive information, or provenance information. The new types of information can be treated as additional metadata attributes associated with each archive. The attributes can be assigned unique names (starting with Archive-), and set as required attributes on the GLOBAL_SIPS or GLOBAL_ARCHIVES collections.

4.3.3.1 *The repository shall have mechanisms for creating, identifying or gathering any extra Representation Information required.*

For example, consider an attribute for a retention period, Archive-Retention. The attribute is set with Policy48, rac-setAIPTemplate.r, by adding a line to the Archive-AIPTemplate file.

C-/lifelibZone/home/rwmoore/Archive-A/SIPS |Archive-Retention |RequiredAIP |

The property is added to each AIP by Policy53, rac-createAIP.r.

The attribute is verified by Policy54, rac-checkAIP.r. Each AIP is examined to verify it has the required metadata specified by attributes defined on GLOBAL_ACCOUNT/*Archive/GLOBAL_ARCHIVES that have the value "RequiredAIP".

Property Creation:

- Policy48 – rac-setAIPTemplate.r

  - Set the name of the AIP template for records in *Archive using the meta-data attribute Archive-AIPTemplate and load the template into the collection GLOBAL_ACCOUNT/*Archive/GLOBAL_REPORTS. This approach assumes that each *Archive holds records that can be processed using a single AIP template. The action is logged in Archive-PAA.

- Policy53 – rac-createAIP.r

  - Loop over all files in the GLOBAL_SIPS directory and copy compliant SIPS (Audit-Comply = "1") to the GLOBAL_ARCHIVES directory. Also set storage location, copy the metadata, set access controls, create the required replicas, and create a handle. A report Archive-AIPCRA is stored in GLOBAL_ACCOUNT/*Archive/GLOBAL_MANIFESTS that documents all problems.

Property Assessment:

- Policy54 – rac-checkAIP.r

  - Loop over all files in the GLOBAL_ARCHIVES directory and verify that each AIP has an Audit-Comply flag with a value of "1". The action results are stored in the Archive-AIPCRA report, stored in GLOBAL_ACCOUNT/*Archive/GLOBAL_MANIFESTS.

4.3.4   THE REPOSITORY SHALL PROVIDE EVIDENCE OF THE EFFECTIVENESS OF ITS PRESERVATION ACTIVITIES

Effectiveness is measured by multiple criteria:

- Completeness. Have preservation policies been applied to all SIPs and AIPs?

- Correctness. Have the policies been correctly applied, and have all errors been handled?

- Consistency. When policies change, have the newest versions been applied to all SIPs and AIPs?

Completeness is enforced by examining every SIP and AIP in verification policies. The policies that operate on AIPs loop over every digital object in the GLOBAL_ARCHIVES collection, process each item, and report anomalies in Archive-PAA, which is stored in GLOBAL_ACCOUNT/*Archive/GLOBAL_MANIFESTS.

Correctness is verified through assessment policies that examine the state information generated by the application of a preservation policy. In many cases, the current state of a digital object can be compared with the required state. Anomalies can be detected and handled. Examples include:

- Integrity checks. The current checksum is compared with the saved checksum in Policy29, rac-verifyIntegrity.r. The results are logged in Archive-RCA.

- Periodic reviews. The Audit-Date attribute on a document is compared with the current date to determine whether a review is needed by Policy7, rac-generateReportStatus.r. The results are logged in Archive-SSA.

- Access controls. The current access controls are compared with required access controls specified by the Archive-IPR attribute in Policy37, rac-verifyIPR.r. The results are logged in Archive-IPA.

- Processing steps. Process result flags are stored for each AIP to denote the preservation processing steps that were completed successfully. Processing status flags are managed by Policy53, rac-createAIP.r, for:

  ○ Checking for duplicates

  ○ Verifying format type

  ○ Checking integrity

  ○ Checking required metadata

  ○ Checking for protected data

  ○ Checking for viruses

  ○ Checking descriptive metadata terms for compliance with a reserved vocabulary.

The results are logged in Archive-AIPCRA.

4.4 AIP PRESERVATION

Preservation is a form of communication with the future. The context, content, management policies, and management actions associated with an AIP have to be communicated into the future for access by a future archivist. The future archivist, in turn, needs to be able to verify assertions made about the original AIP. The future archivist needs to be able to verify authenticity, integrity, chain of custody, and original arrangement. The future archivist also needs to be able to discover an AIP, parse an AIP, and control access to an AIP.

To verify the properties of the AIP, the future archivist needs access to the SIPs, the information content assigned to each AIP, and the reports that document the actions performed upon each AIP. Thus preservation is needed not only for AIPS, but also for the administrative documents.

To support the interpretation of an AIP, representation information is required. There are three approaches:

- Transformative migration, the format is transformed to the representation that can be interpreted by current-day technology.

- Persistent object, the format is kept in the original syntax, but an application that can parse the original format is maintained in a machine image, ensuring the ability to execute the application on current operating systems.

- Emulation, instead of using a virtual machine environment to interface between the original operating system and current operating systems, an emulator is written that maps each operation performed by the original parsing application to the current operating system.

The mechanism that provides the greatest flexibility, fidelity, and preservation capabilities is the persistent object. The archive can encapsulate each original parsing application in a Docker container, and execute the application on future operating systems.

4.4.1   THE REPOSITORY SHALL HAVE SPECIFICATIONS FOR HOW THE AIPS ARE STORED DOWN TO THE BIT LEVEL

Documents are needed to describe the current set of Docker containers that are being managed by the repository, Archive-DIRA, and to describe services that can be used to transform the data format, Archive-BDA.

- Policy67 – rac-listContainers.r

    ○ List the containers that are used to manage preservation services for format transformation, protected data identification, virus detection, indexing, handle generation, reserved vocabulary ontology, and format identification. All containers are located in the collection GLOBAL_ACCOUNT/GLOBAL_REPOSITORY/GLOBAL_IMAGES. A report called Archive-DIRA is created and stored in GLOBAL_ACCOUNT/GLOBAL_REPOSITORY/GLOBAL_MANIFESTS.

- Policy68 – rac-listTransforms.r

     ◦ List the format transformations that can be applied to an AIP (persistent object). The Brown Dog format transformation service is used. A report called Archive-BDA is created and stored in GLOBAL_ACCOUNT/*Archive/GLOBAL_MANIFESTS.

4.4.1.1 *The repository shall preserve the Content Information of AIPs.*

The types of errors that may compromise AIP content information include:

- Operator error (deletion of the AIP by mistake)

- Media failure (disk crash or broken tape)

- Hardware failure (faulty disk controller or bad micro-code in a tape drive)

- Software failure (operating system crash)

- Natural disaster (earthquake, fire, hurricane)

To protect against these failure modes, multiple copies of an AIP are required. The copies should be created on:

- Different types of storage systems

- Located at geographically distant sites

- Managed by different operations teams

- Using different metadata catalogs to manage copies of state information.

Multiple instances of the metadata catalog are also required to ensure that the location of each AIP is known. Replication is controlled by Policy26, rac-setChecksum.re. Each time an AIP is created, it is automatically replicated to sites specified by the replication node, LTLRepl.

```
LTLResc:passthru
  └── LTLRepl:replication
        ├── LTLRenci:unix file system
        └── LTLSils:unix file system
```

Copies are made at both LTLRenci and LTLSils, which are 3.5 miles apart, use different storage technologies, and are managed by different administrators. The metadata catalog is replicated to a third site using Postgresql streaming replication.

4.4.1.2 *The repository shall actively monitor the integrity of AIPs.*

The integrity of AIPS is monitored periodically using Policy29, rac-verifyIntegrity.r. The rule is designed to run every year, calculate a new checksum for each AIP, and compare with the saved value. All anomalies are detected, repaired, and reported to Archive-RCA.

- Policy29 – rac-verifyIntegrity.r

  - Verify the checksum of each file in all of the *Archive collections and replace bad files with a good replica.

  - Note that each of the separate archive collections are checked. A periodic rule is initiated to do the checks yearly. Results are written to GLOBAL_ACCOUNT/GLOBAL_REPOSITORY/GLOBAL_MANIFESTS/Archive-RCA.

4.4.2   THE REPOSITORY SHALL HAVE CONTEMPORANEOUS RECORDS OF ACTIONS AND ADMINISTRATION PROCESSES THAT ARE RELEVANT TO STORAGE AND PRESERVATION OF THE AIPS

Separate manifests are used to document actions and administrative processes for the repository and for a specific Archive within the repository. Actions taken on the repository, such as tracking staff development, are documented in the manifest GLOBAL_ACCOUNT/GLOBAL_REPOSITORY/GLOBAL_MANIFESTS/Archive-RAA. Actions taken on an *Archive are documented in GLOBAL_ACCOUNT/*Archive/GLOBAL_MANIFESTS/Archive-PAA.

4.4.2.1 *The repository shall have procedures for all actions taken on AIPs.*

All actions on AIPs are driven through policies. Specific actions that are applied include:

Policy #	Rule Name	Rule
43	rac-verifyMetadata.r	Verify the attributes on either the SIPS or AIPs
48	rac-setAIPTemplate.r	Set the name of the AIP Template used by an *Archive and load the template
49	rac-verifyAIPTemplate.r	Check that the Audit-AIPTemplate attribute is set and that the Archive-AIP template exists
50	rac-createDIP.r	Package all metadata for an AIP and store as file in GLOBAL_DIPS
51	rac-checkSIP.r	Check SIP for compliance with preservation policies
52	rac-checkAllSIPS.r	Check for non-compliant SIPS

53	rac-createAIP.r	Create AIPs from compliant SIPs
54	rac-checkAIP.r	Verify each AIP has an Audit-Comply flag with value "1"
56	rac-createHandle.r	Create a handle for a file in GLOBAL_ARCHIVES
57	rac-checkHandle.r	Check that a handle exists for every AIP
58	rac-testImmutability.r	Verify that replacing a replica or migrating the file does not affect the persistent identifiers
59	rac-checkDuplicates.r	List all values of Audit-Handle and check for duplicates
60	rac-setFormat.r	Set the DATA_TYPE for an AIP
61	rac-invokeService.r	Generic policy for invoking an external service
62	rac-auditRule.re	Generic rule to apply auditing at each policy enforcement point
64	rac-verifyIntegrityArchive.r	Verify the integrity of all digital objects in *Archive
65	rac-createAudit.r	Query ElasticSearch for audit events
66	rac-checkFormat.r	Check that the format of an AIP complies with Archive-Format
68	rac-listTransforms.r	List possible format transformations that can be applied to an AIP

4.4.2.2 *The repository shall be able to demonstrate that any actions taken on AIPs were compliant with the specification of those actions.*

Two levels of assessment are needed for verifying that the repository appropriately preserves records. Each procedure needs to be checked to verify that the fundamental preservation properties of authenticity, integrity, chain of custody, and original arrangement are maintained. This is illustrated by Policy58, rac-testImmutability.r.

However, even if each procedure works perfectly, there is still the problem of managing failure modes associated with operations, hardware, and software.

To demonstrate that the procedures work correctly, and that the generated properties are preserved in the presence of failure modes, assessment criteria are applied through separate assessment policies. Twenty-eight assessment policies check that a required property is present on each AIP.

Policy #	Rule Name	Rule
3	rac-verifyReportUpdates.r	Verify that updates have been done
6	rac-generateReportNotifications.r	Maintain a manifest of e-mail notifications for management review
10	rac-listRoles.r	List number of staff for each repository role and their names
15	rac-listOntologies.r	List the knowledge communities and associated ontologies
18	rac-listPolicies.r	Retrieve most recent version of policies registered into the metadata catalog
19	rac-listMicroservices.r	Retrieve most recent version of micro-services registered into the metadata catalog
20	rac-listAttributes	List the preservation attributes updated by preservation policies
22	rac-listAuditEvents.r	List the audit events, including version number and date
24	rac-verifyPublicAccess.r	Verify public access on the GLOBAL_REPOSITORY collection
25	rac-listRulebase.r	List the current rule base and create a report
27	rac-checkNumberReplicas.r	Update the manifest file "Archive-RC" with a list of all missing replicas
28	rac-updateReplicas.r	Update all replicas through a rebalance operation
29	rac-verifyIntegrity.r	Verify checksum of each file in GLOBAL_ARCHIVES
32	rac-listAccess.r	List persons who have access to an archives
37	rac-verifyIPR.r	Verify IPR based access controls on an archives
40	rac-verifySource.r	Verify presence of required metadata on SIPS
43	rac-verifyMetadata.r	Verify the attributes on either the SIPS or AIPs
47	rac-verifyAttribute.r	Send a notification when checking attributes on *Archive (mod to Policy43)
49	rac-verifyAIPTemplate.r	Check that the Audit-AIPTemplate attribute is set and that the Archive-AIP template exists
51	rac-checkSIP.r	Check SIP for compliance with preservation policies
54	rac-checkAIP.r	Verify each AIP has an Audit-Comply flag with value "1"

57	rac-checkHandle.r	Check that a handle exists for every AIP
58	rac-testImmutability.r	Verify that replacing a replica or migrating the file does not affect the persistent identifiers
59	rac-checkDuplicates.r	List all values of Audit-Handle and check for duplicates
63	rac-checkVocab.r	Check all SIPs for Audit-CheckVocab attribute set to "1" and send notification
64	rac-verifyIntegrityArchive.r	Verify the integrity of all digital objects in *Archive
65	rac-createAudit.r	Query ElasticSearch for audit events
66	rac-checkFormat.r	Check that the format of an AIP complies with Archive-Format

4.5   INFORMATION MANAGEMENT

The identification of material of interest can be achieved through multiple contexts:

- Original arrangement. The order in a record series can be used. Each record series is managed in the repository as a separate sub-collection of an *Archive. This makes it possible to browse for an AIP based on related AIPs in a record series.

- Unique handle. Given a handle, a query can be issued to retrieve the AIP and associated descriptive information. This is done in Policy69, rac-getAIP.r.

  ○ Policy69 – Find an AIP based on its handle or uniqueID

    • Given a handle, find the corresponding AIP and the associated descriptive information. The name of the *Archive is derived, and the access is logged to GLOBAL_ACCOUNT/*Archive/GLOBAL_MANIFESTS/Archive-PAA.

- Descriptive information. Each AIP has a set of metadata attributes that provides a context, Audit-Description. A query can be made on a term in the description, Audit-Description, using Policy70, rac-getAIPfromDescription.r, to identify an AIP.

  ○ Policy70 – Use a term in Audit-Description to get information about an AIP.

    • Given a term in Audit-Description, find the corresponding AIP and the associated descriptive information. The name of the *Archive is derived, and the access is logged to GLOBAL_ACCOUNT/*Archive/GLOBAL_MANIFESTS/Archive-PAA.

- Metadata indexing. The ElasticSearch system is used to index all descriptive metadata terms, Audit-Description. Policy71, rac-indexArchive.r, manages the indexing. Policy72, rac-getAIPfromIndex.r, returns an AIP given a descriptive term.

  ○ Policy71 – Index the descriptive metadata terms in an *Archive.

    - An external ElasticSearch service is invoked to index the descriptive metadata in a specified *Archive. This is an example policy for initiating an index. The action is logged to GLOBAL_ACCOUNT/*Archive/GLOBAL_MANIFESTS/Archive-PAA.

  ○ Policy72 – Return information about an AIP given a descriptive term by querying an index.

    - A full text index can be made in ElasticSearch of the metadata used to describe AIPs in an archive. A query is issued against the index to find AIPs that use the term, and the access is logged to GLOBAL_ACCOUNT/*Archive/GLOBAL_MANIFESTS/Archive-PAA.

4.5.1   THE REPOSITORY SHALL SPECIFY MINIMUM INFORMATION REQUIREMENTS TO ENABLE THE DESIGNATED COMMUNITY TO DISCOVER AND IDENTIFY MATERIAL OF INTEREST

The Archive-SIP document specifies the description information required for each SIP. These descriptive terms are copied onto the AIP when it is formed by Poliicy53, rac-createAIP.r.

4.5.2   THE REPOSITORY SHALL CAPTURE OR CREATE MINIMUM DESCRIPTIVE INFORMATION AND ENSURE THAT IT IS ASSOCIATED WITH THE AIP

Policy-41, rac-setMetadata.r, adds the required metadata to the collection GLOBAL_ACCOUNT/*Archive/GLOBAL_SIPS. Policy51, rac-checkSIP.r, checks that the description is present on each SIP. Note that the description can be composed from multiple lines of text, each of which is associated with a SIP through the attribute name Audit-Description. The descriptive metadata can be checked for each AIP with Policy79, rac-checkDescription.r. The output is written to the report GLOBAL_ACCOUNT/*Archive/GLOBAL_REPORTS/Archive-MA, the descriptive metadata report.

Property Creation:

- Policy41 – rac-setMetadata.r

∘ Read a pipe-delimited metadata file and set the required SIP metadata attributes on a specified collection name. The format of the file is

C-/lifelibZone/home/rwmoore/Archive-A/SIPS |Audit-Depositor |RequiredSIP |
C-/lifelibZone/home/rwmoore/Archive-A/SIPS |Audit-Source |RequiredSIP |
C-/lifelibZone/home/rwmoore/Archive-A/SIPS |Archive-Format |RequiredSIP |
C-/lifelibZone/home/rwmoore/Archive-A/SIPS |Archive-IPR |RequiredSIP |
C-/lifelibZone/home/rwmoore/Archive-A/SIPS |Archive-Ontology |RequiredSIP |
C-/lifelibZone/home/rwmoore/Archive-A/SIPS |Archive-Description |RequiredSIP |

The action is logged in Archive-PAA.

Property Assessment:

- Policy51 – rac-checkSIP.r

  ∘ Checks a SIP for compliance with preservation policies. The policy function rac-CheckMetadata is invoked to verify the terms used within Audit-Description are consistent with terms listed in the knowledge ontology. The action is logged in Archive-PAA.

- Policy79 – rac-checkDescription.r

  ∘ Checks that descriptive metadata, Audit-Description, is assigned to every AIP. A report, Archive-MA, is created for all non-compliant AIPs and stored in GLOBAL_ACCOUNT/*Archive/GLOBAL_REPORTS.

4.5.3 THE REPOSITORY SHALL MAINTAIN BI-DIRECTIONAL LINKAGE BETWEEN EACH AIP AND ITS DESCRIPTIVE INFORMATION

Each AIP is stored in multiple vaults, using a path name that is dependent upon the type of storage device. To ensure that a bi-directional linkage can be maintained between the AIP and the descriptive metadata, it is necessary to be able to find the description using the physical path name of the AIP. This is made possible by appending the AIP logical name to the vault path name.

For example, given the collection and file name of a record, the logical path name is

GLOBAL_ACCOUNT/*Archive/GLOBAL_ARCHIVES/record-name

The physical path name on the storage vault is then constructed from:

Vault-path-name/GLOBAL_ACCOUNT/*Archive/GLOBAL_ARCHIVES/record-name

The logical path name can then be found by stripping the Vault-path-name. A query can then be made on either the ElasticSearch index or the metadata catalog to retrieve the descriptive information. A query can also be made on the Descriptive Information to find the logical names of the AIPS.

The policy enforcement point rule,

acSetVaultPathPolicy {msiSetGraftPathScheme("no","1"); }

enforces the construction of the physical path name from the logical path name.

The opposite linkage direction is supported. Given the logical name of an AIP, the descriptive information can be retrieved. This is shown in Policy50, rac-createDIP.r. The attributes that are listed include the physical path name and the descriptive metadata.

4.5.3.1 *The repository shall maintain the associations between its AIPs and their descriptive information over time.*

The metadata attributes stored in the metadata catalog are directly linked to each AIP through internal data grid identifiers:

DATA_ID	Internal identifier for each file
META_DATA_ATTR_ID	Internal identifier for each metadata attribute associated with a file
COLL_ID	Internal identifier for each collection
META_COLL_ATTR_ID	Internal identifier for each metadata attribute associated with a collection

An internal table maps a metadata ID to a DATA_ID or a COLL_ID. This link is preserved as long as the file or collection exists. Note that this approach makes it possible for a given META_DATA_ATTR_ID to be associated with multiple files. A META_COLL_ATTR_ID can also be associated with multiple collections. The persistence of these links is verified by Policy58, rac-testImmutability.r.

4.6   ACCESS MANAGEMENT

Documents that support access management include:

Access log	Archive-ALA	ISO 4.6.1
Access Failure report	Archive-AFA	ISO 4.6.1.1
DIP template for required metadata	Archive-DIP	ISO 4.6.2
Error reports	Archive-ERR	ISO 4.6.2.1

4.6.1   THE REPOSITORY SHALL COMPLY WITH ACCESS POLICIES

Data grids enforce access controls on files and collections. Every access is authenticated and every operation is authorized. Data grid internal state information is used to enforce the access controls:

USER_ID	Unique internal identifier for a user
USER_NAME	Account name associated with a user
DATA_ID	Unique internal identifier for a file
COLL_ID	Unique internal identifier for a collection
DATA_ACCESS_USER_ID	User ID who has access to a file
DATA_ACCESS_DATA_ID	File ID that the DATA_ACCESS_USER_ID can access
DATA_ACCESS_TYPE	Identifier for the type of access
COLL_ACCESS_USER_ID	User ID who has access to a collection
COLL_ACCESS_COLL_ID	Collection ID that the COLL_ACCESS_USER_ID can access
COLL_ACCESS_TYPE	Identifier for the type of access

For a given DATA_ID, a query can be issued to retrieve the DATA_ACCESS_TYPE and DATA_ACCESS_USER_ID where the DATA_ACCESS_DATA_ID is equal to the DATA_ID. This defines which users can access a file.

Access policies are set up by Policy33, rac-setIPR.r. This sets access controls to restrict access to persons who own the intellectual property. Access controls are verified by Policy37, rac-verify-IPR.r. Access controls are changed by Policy34, rac-resetIPR.r.

Accesses are logged through the audit system. File access events are written to an external indexing system, ElasticSearch. The time and account are registered. The Access Log report, Archive-ALA, is generated by Policy73, rac-getAccessfromIndex.r, which queries ElasticSearch to retrieve events related to access.

Property Creation:

- Policy73 – rac-getAccessfromIndex.r

    ○ A query is issued to ElasticSearch to return all access events. This is a variation of Policy72, rac-getAIPfromIndex.r, which returns access information instead of description information. The result is written to a report, GLOBAL_ACCOUNT/*Archive/GLOBAL_REPORTS/Archive-ALA.

4.6.1.1 The repository shall log and review all access management failures and anomalies.

A variation of Policy73, rac-getAccessfromIndex.r, is rac-getAccessFailuresfromIndex.r which only returns failed access events. A query is made to ElasticSearch to identify all access failures. A report is created called Archive-AFA, Access Failure report.

Property Creation:

- Policy74 – rac-getAccessFailuresfromIndex.r

    ○ A query is issued to ElasticSearch to return all access failure events. This is a variation of Policy73, rac-getAccessfromIndex.r, which returns failed accesses instead of all accesses. The result is written to a report, GLOBAL_ACCOUNT/*Archive/GLOBAL_MANIFESTS/Archive-AFA.

4.6.2   THE REPOSITORY SHALL FOLLOW POLICIES AND PROCEDURES THAT ENABLE THE DISSEMINATION OF DIGITAL OBJECTS THAT ARE TRACEABLE TO THE ORIGINALS, WITH EVIDENCE SUPPORTING THEIR AUTHENTICITY

Dissemination of DIPS corresponds to the creation of a metadata file that contains all information related to authenticity, description, and representation. This is done by Policy50, rac-createDIP.r. The DIP metadata file is stored in GLOBAL_ACCOUNT/*Archive/GLOBAL_DIPS/dip-file-name. The name of the DIP file is created by appending "-meta" to the name of the AIP.

The required metadata for a DIP is assumed to be the same as the required metadata for an AIP. Thus copying all of the AIP information about authenticity, description, and representation will generate a viable DIP. The required metadata is documented in an externally generated report, Archive-DIP, which is stored in GLOBAL_ACCOUNT/*Archive/GLOBAL_REPORTS. The report is managed by Policy3-Policy8, Policy26, Policy35, and Policy36.

4.6.2.1 The repository shall record and act upon problem reports about errors in data or responses from users.

Reports about errors in data and responses from users are documented in an externally generated report, Archive-ERR. The report is implemented as a Manifest to which new errors can be added. The responses to error reports will generate actions that are logged in Archive-RAA for repository concerns or Archive-PAA for *Archive concerns. The Archive-ERR report is stored in GLOBAL_ACCOUNT/GLOBAL_REPOSITORY/GLOBAL_MANIFESTS. The report is managed by Policy3-Policy8, Policy26, Policy35, and Policy36.

CHAPTER 5

ISO 16363 Infrastructure and Security Risk Management

Section 5 of the ISO 16363 standard identifies requirements for managing the infrastructure (both hardware and software components), and for managing risk.

The infrastructure used to implement the repository requires maintenance, upgrades, and evaluation to minimize risks associated with obsolescence, failure modes, and malicious attacks.

Documents that support technical infrastructure risk management include:

Corruption reports	Archive-RCA	ISO 3.3.5
Infrastructure List report	Archive-ILA	ISO 5.1.1
Technology Watch report	Archive-TW	ISO 5.1.1.1
Usage report	Archive-URA	ISO 5.1.1.1.2
Technology Change report	Archive-PL	ISO 5.1.1.1.3
Test System Evaluation report	Archive-TSE	ISO 5.1.1.1.4
Audit of Performance	Archive-APU	ISO 5.1.1.1.6
Security Patch report	Archive-PR	ISO 5.1.1.4
Traceability report (operations/state)	Archive-TRA	ISO 5.1.1.6
Change Management report	Archive-CM	ISO 5.1.1.6.1

5.1 TECHNICAL INFRASTRUCTURE RISK MANAGEMENT

The technical infrastructure is comprised of multiple components that need to evolve to track emerging standards, minimize cost of maintenance, and take advantage of improvements in storage capacity, access rates, and computational rates. The software components include:

- **iRODS data grid** – manage the properties of a distributed collection, including persistent naming, arrangement, distribution, retention, disposition, aggregation, access controls, authentication, auditing.

- **iRODS pluggable rule engine** – execute the policies controlling the collection and manage the rule base.

- **iRODS technology plugins** – manage interactions with authentication systems, storage systems, network protocols, micro-services, and clients.

- **QueryArrow** – manage virtualization of metadata, the ability to distribute metadata across information repositories, apply access controls, and optimize interactions.

- **Metadata catalog** – store the state information for the data grid and the preservation metadata attributes.

- **Discovery Environment** – manage virtualization of services in Docker containers to enable migration of services across operating systems.

- **Services in Docker containers** – ElasticSearch for indexing, BrownDog for format transformation, PRONOM for format type detection, clamscan for virus detection, BitCurator for protected data identification, Handle for persistent identifiers, HT-Condor for queued execution of workflows.

The hardware components include:

- **Storage systems** – Unix file systems, NetApp clustered data, Quantum StorNext hierarchical storage manager

- **Computer servers** – Cloud, Unix clusters

- **Networks** – Exo-GENI, Internet2.

5.1.1 THE REPOSITORY SHALL IDENTIFY AND MANAGE THE RISKS TO ITS PRESERVATION OPERATIONS AND GOALS ASSOCIATED WITH SYSTEM INFRASTRUCTURE

An infrastructure component list, Archive-ILA, documents the type and version of each software and hardware component. The document is stored in GLOBAL_ACCOUNT/GLOBAL_REPOSITORY/GLOBAL_REPORTS. The information provided by Archive-ILA includes:

Operations – list of system components
Operations – estimates of system component lifetime
Operations – identification of community supported software

The report is generated by the iRODS icommand, izonereport.

izonereport > Archive-ILA

This utility queries the entire iRODS data grid for configuration information, and formats the results using JSON. The configuration is validated against schemas registered at https://schemas.irods.org. The lifetime of each component is determined by the version number associated with the component plugin. New versions are released and documented in the published schemas. This provides a simple way to track required evolution of the system. The report contains:

1. Name of schema used to evaluate the configuration, https://schemas.iRODS.org/configuration/v2/zone_bundle.json;

2. The build information including operating system, complier versions, and iRODS version;

3. The plug-ins used for interactions with technologies, including a checksum for each plug-in;

4. The storage configuration, including the location and type of each storage device, and a count of the number of stored objects;

5. The internal iRODS map files for assigning variable names and the map file for assigning micro-service names;

6. The rule base;

7. The database configuration file;

8. The rules for interacting with a message bus;

9. The policy functions; and

10. The server configuration including all iRODS system parameters.

Items 2–10 are repeated for each server in the data grid. This information is sufficient to rebuild the entire data grid infrastructure.

A separate set of Ansible scripts are used to rebuild the Discovery Environment and the services in the Docker containers.

An externally created document identifies the risk associated with each technology component. The report is called Archive-IRL and is stored in GLOBAL_ACCOUNT/GLOBAL_REPOSITORY/GLOBAL_REPORTS.

5.1.1.1 *The repository shall employ technology watches or other technology monitoring notification systems.*

The infrastructure components used by the repository consist of community-supported open source software systems that are available on Github.com.

- **iRODS** – provided by the iRODS Consortium, http://irods.org.

- **Discovery Environment** – provided by Cyverse, http://cyverse.org.

- **Clamscan** – provided by NPM, https://www.npmjs.com/package/clamscan.

- **HIVE** – provided by the Metadata Research Center, http://cci.drexel.edu/mrc/projects/hive/.

- **ElasticSearch** – provided on Github, https://github.com/elastic/elasticsearch.

- **BitCurator** – provided by the BitCurator consortium, http://www.bitcurator.net.

- **PRONOM** – provided by the National Archives, http://www.nationalarchives.gov.uk/PRONOM/Default.aspx.

- **BrownDog** – provided by NCSA, http://browndog.ncsa.illinois.edu.

- **Handle** – provided by the Corporation for National Research Initiatives, https://www.handle.net.

- **HTCondor** – provided by the University of Wisconsin–Madison, https://www.google.com/search?client=safari&rls=en&q=HTCondor&ie=UTF-8&oe=UTF-8.

Technology monitoring is tracked through the new releases provided by each group. Since iRODS uses a pluggable architecture, new technologies can be added to the system by developing a new plug-in. This makes it possible to identify and incorporate new technology by watching for new plug-ins provided by the iRODS Consortium.

A Technology Watch Report, Archive-TW, is generated externally by monitoring the listed websites. The report is stored in GLOBAL_ACCOUNT/GLOBAL_REPOSITORY/GLOBAL_REPORTS and contains:

Operations – Analysis comparing existing technology to each new assessment

The report is managed by Policy3-Policy8, Policy26, Policy35, and Policy36.

5.1.1.1.1   The repository shall have hardware technologies appropriate to the services it provides to its designated communities.

The choice of hardware technology is driven by cost, capacity, access rates, and reliability. Since the data grid manages distributed storage servers, new storage systems can be added without affecting the current system. Data and metadata can be migrated to the new systems without affecting operation.

5.1.1.1.2   The repository shall have procedures in place to monitor and receive notifications when hardware technology changes are needed.

The determination when hardware technology changes are needed does require monitoring the amount of data stored, the access rate, and the observed data transfer rates. Storage usage is provided by Policy38, rac-surveyArchive.r. The access rate is monitored by the database and is controlled by the number of connection ports. The network performance is monitored by data transport measurements between selected sites.

A usage report, Archive-URA, is generated by a query to the auditing system to track the number of files that are accessed and their size. The result is stored in GLOBAL_ACCOUNT/*Archive/GLOBAL_REPORTS.

- Policy75 – rac-getUsagefromIndex.r

  ◦ A query is issued to ElasticSearch to return the number of files that are accessed and their size. Policy75, rac-getUsagefromIndex.r, is a variation of Policy73, rac-getAccessFailuresfromIndex.r, which returns the usage instead of the failed accesses. The result is written to a report, GLOBAL_ACCOUNT/*Archive/GLOBAL_REPORTS/Archive-URA.

5.1.1.1.3   The repository shall have procedures in place to evaluate when changes are needed to current hardware.

When the usage rate becomes a substantial fraction of the capacity of a system, then new technology will be needed. This may be either an entirely new system, requiring a migration from the old system to the new system, or additional servers based on the current technology to expand capacity. The choice is based on the system that has minimal capital and operating cost.

The current system plug ins are documented in Archive-ILA. The report is versioned, enabling the tracking of changes to each plug-in. The evaluation criteria for changes in technology are logged in an externally generated report, Archive-PL. This documents the choice of new hardware, and the motivation for switching from the current systems. The report is stored in

GLOBAL_ACCOUNT/GLOBAL_REPOSITORY/GLOBAL_MANIFESTS and is managed by Policy3-Policy8, Policy26, Policy35, and Policy36. The Archive-PL report contains:

Operations – Evaluation procedures for selecting new technology
Operations – Documentation of staff expertise with selected technology
Operations – Motivation for switching to new technology
Operations – Contracted level of service
Operations – Commitment to provide the contracted level of service
Operations – Financial assets set aside for hardware procurement
Operations – Demonstrations of cost savings
Operations – Evaluation procedures for selecting new technology
Operations – Documentation of staff expertise with selected technology
Operations – Motivation for switching to new technology

5.1.1.1.4   The repository shall have procedures, commitment and funding to replace hardware when evaluation indicates the need to do so.

Procedures for replacing hardware include:

- Evaluation of the hardware in a test system. This requires installation of the entire repository infrastructure on the test system, the addition of the plug-ins that interact with the new technology, and the execution of test scripts that evaluate correct operation. Test scripts are downloaded from Github:

  - https://github.com/irods/irods_testing_provisioner_vsphere

  - https://github.com/irods/irods_testing_zone_bundle

  - https://github.com/irods/irods_testing_jargon

- A report, Archive-TSE, is generated from the tests, which documents the results of each of the test scripts. The report is stored in GLOBAL_ACCOUNT/GLOBAL_REPOSITORY/GLOBAL_REPORTS and is managed by Policy3-Policy8, Policy26, Policy35, and Policy36. The report contains:

Operations – Test procedures used for evaluation
Operations – Results of test procedures
Operations – Comparison with prior technology

The choice of new technology is driven primarily by capital and operating cost. If the new system is lower in cost for the same capacity and performance, then replacement of the hardware lowers the cost of the repository.

However, if the choice of new technology is driven by a requirement to increase capacity, then increased funding from the users of the repository is required. Note that capital costs for storage are well defined for a record. Each new generation of storage technology typically provides twice the storage capacity per media while keeping the cost of the new media the same as the prior technology. This means the total media cost for storage of a record across all technology upgrades increases by a factor of $1 + \frac{1}{2} + \frac{1}{4} + \ldots = 2$ over the original media cost. If migration to new storage systems is automated using policies, and administrative functions are automated using policies, the cost for storing a record indefinitely is twice the media cost plus utility costs plus floor space cost plus maintenance costs.

5.1.1.1.5 The repository shall have software technologies appropriate to the services it provides to its designated communities.

The software services provided by the repository are supported by the iRODS data grid and the functions registered into the Discovery Environment as Docker containers. The set of services include:

Naming	iROD file DATA_NAME
Arrangement	iRODS collection COLL_NAME
Authentication	iRODS plug-in, PAM
Authorization	iRODS DATA_ACCESS USER_ID, DATA_ACCESS_DATA_ID, DATA_ACCESS_TYPE
Distribution	iRODS storage, RESC_HIER
Discovery	iRODS metadata, META_DATA_ATTR_NAME
Indexing	Docker image, ElasticSearch
Auditing	iRODS audit trail
Persistent ID	Docker image, Handle
Protected data discovery	Docker image, BitCurator
Virus detection	Docker image, clamscan
Workflow execution	Discovery Environment, HTCondor
Format identification	Docker image, PRONOM
Format transformation	Docker image, BrownDog
Reserved vocabulary	Docker image, HIVE
Domain registry	Docker image, DataONE member node

The set of services can be augmented by adding Docker containers that encapsulate a new service, by accessing external services through a web service protocol encapsulated in an iRODS policy, by writing a policy to invoke a service through a message bus, or by writing a plug-in driver for directly executing the protocol required by the new service. Interactions with each service can be audited, or captured as metadata associated with each AIP.

5.1.1.1.6 The repository shall have procedures in place to monitor and receive notifications when software changes are needed.

Software changes are driven either by requirements for new features, or by issues with performance. Notifications for required changes primarily come from the user community, through requests for bug fixes, or new capabilities, or identification of performance problems.

An externally generated report for the Audit of Performance, Archive-APU, documents the requests. The report is partially based on issues submitted to the iRODS Github account, https://github.com/issues. The current areas in Github include change requests for documentation, setup, logging, configuration, change log, and clients. The Archive-APU report is stored in GLOBAL_ACCOUNT/GLOBAL_REPOSITORY/GLOBAL_REPORTS and is managed by Policy3-Policy8, Policy26, Policy35, and Policy36. The report contains:

Operations – Feature requests
Operations – Bug reports
Operations – Change requests for documentation, setup, logging, configuration, change log, and clients

5.1.1.1.7 The repository shall have procedures in place to evaluate when changes are needed to current software.

The procedures that evaluate when changes are needed to software include:

- Policy29, rac-verifyIntegrity.r, which documents data corruption;

- Policy38, rac-surveyArchive.r, which generates storage usage;

- Policy73, rac-getAccessfromIndex.r, which tracks accesses; and

- Policy75, rac-getUsagefromIndex.r, which tracks usage.

The reports that document the evaluations include:

- Archive-SEA, staff experience audit to track expertise across systems;

- Archive-RCA, replica check report;

- Archive-CIRA, Content Information Deposition Report;

- Archive-ALA, Access log;

- Archive-URA, Usage report; and

- Archive-APU, Audit of Performance with user requests. This report drives changes to software to support new features.

5.1.1.1.8   The repository shall have procedures, commitment and funding to replace software when evaluation indicates the need to do so.

Software replacement is done through procedures similar to hardware replacement.

- Evaluation of the software in a test system. This requires installation of the entire repository infrastructure on the test system, the addition of the plug-ins that interact with the hardware, and the execution of test scripts that evaluate correct operation. Test scripts are downloaded from Github:

  ○ https://github.com/irods/irods_testing_provisioner_vsphere

  ○ https://github.com/irods/irods_testing_zone_bundle

  ○ https://github.com/irods/irods_testing_jargon

- A report, Archive-TSE, is generated from the tests, which documents the results of each of the test scripts. The report is stored in GLOBAL_ACCOUNT/GLOBAL_REPOSITORY/GLOBAL_REPORTS and is managed by Policy3-Policy8, Policy26, Policy35, and Policy36. The report contains:

Operations – Test procedures used for evaluation
Operations – Results of test procedures
Operations – Comparison with prior technology

By building on open source software systems, the cost of acquisition of new software is minimized, provided there are automated installation scripts and automated testing procedures to evaluate the systems.

The major motivation for software upgrades is to remain consistent with the most recent releases of the open source software. This ensures that the technology is continually being refreshed, that new capabilities are being added, and that bugs are being fixed.

5.1.1.2 *The repository shall have adequate hardware and software support for backup functionality sufficient for preserving the repository content and tracking repository functions.*

The backup mechanisms are built into the data grid software. The mechanisms include:

- support for data replication across multiple storage systems, including both tape drives and disk arrays;

- support for versioning of changed files;

- support for replication of the metadata catalog to an off-site location. This is critical as the metadata catalog contains the relationships that link preservation metadata to AIPs. The metadata catalog contains information related to access controls, location of replicas, and checksum values. Audit trail information is stored in ElasticSearch; and

- support for dumps of the metadata catalog. This is a second level of redundancy for management of metadata.

Documentation of backups is contained in multiple reports:

- Archive-RAA, Repository Action report

- Archive-RCA, Replica check report

- Archive-PAA, Preservation Action Audit report

- Archive-ARUA, Audit report of all actions.

These reports document the events associated with backup activities, and also document the existence of multiple copies of each AIP. For each AIP, a DIP metadata report documents the location of each replica.

5.1.1.3 *The repository shall have effective mechanisms to detect bit corruption or loss.*

Periodic analysis of the integrity of the repository holdings is done by Policy29, rac-verifyIntegrity.r. The policy checks that each replica has a correct checksum, deletes corrupted replicas, and runs a rebalance operation to replace missing replicas. The rebalance operation is applied to all files stored in the replication resource and guarantees that the replica is present on each resource within the replication hierarchy. The results are logged in Archive-RCA.

5.1.1.3.1 *The repository shall record and report to its administration all incidents of data corruption or loss, and steps shall be taken to repair/replace corrupt or lost data.*

The detection of corruption events is logged by Policy29, rac-verifyIntegrity.r, in

GLOBAL_ACCOUNT/GLOBAL_REPOSITORY/GLOBAL_REPORTS/Archive-RCA.

Policy29 automatically repairs all corrupted digital objects when they are detected. The frequency with which the detection and repair is done can be increased if the error rate increases. The current detection interval is set at one year.

5.1.1.4 *The repository shall have a process to record and react to the availability of new security updates based on a risk-benefit assessment.*

Security updates are mandated by the institution that houses the repository. The security updates are traditionally targeted at the operating system, but security updates may be needed for clients, libraries, tools, and cyberinfrastructure.

The more general problem is coordinating updates of software across a distributed environment, whether the updates are done for security patches, or bug fixes, or addition of new features. The problem is handled by tracking the version of each software component, analyzing the consistency of the components across storage locations (using the izonereport), and updating each system. This approach is possible provided the technologies are backward compatible, implying that the new version is able to interact with the old version for the subset of features that have not changed.

Some updates are mandated by the institution that require the replacement of the operating system. This requires the installation of the entire cyberinfrastructure stack on the new operating system. This is managed by an installation script that automates the process. An implication is that in many cases the security patch is done independently of the repository, with the repository re-installed on top of the updated system. This approach is a general solution to the problem of updates: Given the revised system, re-install the repository infrastructure. This approach is also used to install new versions of the repository itself. The installation scripts for iRODS are documented at https://docs.irods.org/master/manual/installation/.

The repository augments these installation scripts with the specific policies defined in this document, which are loaded as an additional rule base for controlling the environment.

A security patch report, Archive-PR, is generated externally to track all updates related to security patches. The report is stored in GLOBAL_ACCOUNT/GLOBAL_REPOSITORY/GLOBAL_REPORTS and is managed with Policy3-Policy8, Policy26, Policy35, and Policy36. The report contains:

Operations – Documentation of all available security patches and analysis of their risk
Operations – History of all update installations
Operations – History of update procedures

5.1.1.5 *The repository shall have defined processes for storage media and/or hardware change (e.g., refreshing, migration).*

The migration of data across storage systems is accomplished by adding a storage server as an additional storage resource to a replication node, and then running a rebalance operation. This will automatically create a copy of every file on the new resource. The old resource can then be removed.

Consider the current replication node:

LTLResc:passthru
└── LTLRepl:replication
    ├── LTLRenci:unix file system
    └── LTLSils:unix file system

Adding a new resource, say LTLUnc, changes the replication node storage structure to:

LTLResc:passthru
└── LTLRepl:replication
    ├── LTLRenci:unix file system
    └── LTLSils:unix file system
    └── LTLUnc:unix file system

Applying the rebalance operation forces a replica to be made on LTLUnc. A prior resource can now be removed while preserving two replicas for each file.

LTLResc:passthru
└── LTLRepl:replication
    └── LTLSils:unix file system
    └── LTLUnc:unix file system

5.1.1.6 *The repository shall have identified and documented critical processes that affect its ability to comply with its mandatory responsibilities.*

A Traceability report, Archive-TRA, documents the critical processes that must be preserved for the repository to function. An analysis of repositories based on data grid technology identifies the following key infrastructure components.

- Metadata catalog (information repository). The data grid manages distributed state information by creating a central catalog that holds all preservation metadata and data grid state information. If this catalog is compromised, then the system may lose essential information needed to track authenticity, identify AIP location, manage access controls, etc.

- Rule base (knowledge repository). All policies are stored in the rule base. If the rule base is compromised, the system may not be able to enforce required procedures for preserving authenticity, chain of custody, integrity, and original arrangement.

All other technologies are pluggable, enabling the insertion of new versions of the technology while the repository continues to function. Note that even the rule engine is pluggable, enabling the use of alternate rule languages for the creation of policies.

Given a copy of the metadata catalog, a copy of the rule base, and a copy of the configuration file, the entire system can be re-installed, re-started, and pick up execution from the last prior operation. This includes rules that have been queued for delayed execution, and rules that run periodically.

The Traceability report, Archive-TRA, is stored in GLOBAL_ACCOUNT/*Archive/GLOBAL_REPORTS/Archive-TRA. The report identifies the set of operations and state transitions that are generated by preservation operations. These define a complete description of the processes applied within the repository. The report contains:

Operations – Lists the actions generated by clients
Operations – Lists the policies enforced in the rule base
Operations – Lists the operations executed by the policies
Operations – Maps the operations to persistent state transitions
Operations – Maps the actions to persistent state transitions

The process information is extracted from the Audit trail by Policy76, rac-getProcessfromIndex.r.

- Policy76 – rac-getProcessfromIndex.r

  ○ A query is issued to ElasticSearch to return the state changes generated by a process. The policy, rac-getProcessfromIndex.r, is a variation of Policy73, rac-getAccessFailuresfromIndex.r, which returns process information instead of failed accesses. The result is written to a report, GLOBAL_ACCOUNT/*Archive/GLOBAL_REPORTS/Archive-TRA.

5.1.1.6.1   The repository shall have a documented change management process that identifies changes to critical processes that potentially affect the repository's ability to comply with its mandatory responsibilities.

A Change Management report, Archive-CM, documents all changes to the infrastructure. The change management process includes the steps:

- install the updated software on a test system;

- run the feature verification tests to prove the critical processes work correctly;

- install the updated system on each of the servers within the data grid;

- run the izonereport to document the new versions of the software and generate a new Archive-ILA infrastructure report;

- run Policy53, rac-checkAIP.r, to verify preservation metadata are correct and log the results in Archive-AIPCRA; and

- run Policy29, rac-verifyIntegrity.r, to verify the AIP content is correct and log the results in Archive-RCA.

The report, Archive-CM, documents each step and is stored in GLOBAL_ACCOUNT/GLOBAL_REPOSITORY/GLOBAL_REPORTS and is managed by Policy3-Policy8, Policy26, Policy35, and Policy36. The report contains:

Operations – Analysis of logs of changes for impact
Operations – Analysis of risk associated with a process change
Operations – Analysis of the expected impact of a process change
Operations – Documentation of change management process

5.1.1.6.2   The repository shall have a process for testing and evaluating the effect of changes to the repository's critical processes.

A repository is provably correct when it is possible to do the following steps:

- Identify the actions generated by user clients of the repository

- Map the actions to the preservation policies that are invoked at policy enforcement points

- Identify the operations performed by each policy

- Identify the state changes that are made by each operation

- Verify that state changes can be tracked back to the originating action

- Analyze the state changes to show that the result is consistent with the original action.

Through use of the QueryArrow metadata virtualization system, it is possible to verify each of the steps listed above. The verification needs to be done each time a component of the infrastructure is changed. The process is a generic solution to correctness, and can be applied to the specific instance of preservation policies.

The results of the analysis are saved in the Process Verification Report, Archive-QAR. The report is stored in GLOBAL_ACCOUNT/GLOBAL_REPOSITORY/GLOBAL_REPORTS and managed by Policy3-Policy8, Policy26, Policy35, and Policy36. The report contains:

Operations – Documented testing procedures for critical processes
Operations – Documentation of results from prior tests
Operations – Documentation of changes made as a result of tests
Operations – Analysis of the impact of a process change

5.1.2 THE REPOSITORY SHALL MANAGE THE NUMBER AND LOCATION OF COPIES OF ALL DIGITAL OBJECTS

The iRODS data grid manages persistent state information for every digital object that is stored. These attributes are:

DATA_NAME	Logical name associated with a digital object
DATA_RESC_NAME	Logical name of the storage resource where the digital object is stored
DATA_REPL_NUM	Replica number. As replicas are created this number is incremented.
DATA_REPL_STATUS	Whether the replica has been modified
DATA_MODIFY_TIME	Date when the digital object was modified

These attributes are controlled by the policies:

- Policy26 – rac-setChecksum.re

  ○ This replicates each file, generates a checksum, and sets an audit date. The action is logged in the audit trail.

- Policy29 – rac-verifyIntegrity.r

  ○ This verifies the required number of replicas, and recreates missing replicas. The results are logged in Archive-RCA.

The storage location is controlled by the definition of the replication resource. Each file is replicated to each leaf storage node used by the replication resource.

5.1.2.1 *The repository shall have mechanisms in place to ensure any/multiple copies of digital objects are synchronized.*

Two preservation policy functions control synchronization when reports are updated or extended.

racSaveFile	automatically versions each file when a change is made, and replicates the versioned file
racWriteManifest	adds text to a file, creates a new checksum, and replicates the changed file

The rebalance operation for replication nodes identifies which replica has the most recent DATA_MODIFY_TIME, and uses this replica as the source for synchronizing replicas. This ensures that when replicas are updated, a revised file will not be overwritten by an older file.

5.2 SECURITY RISK MANAGEMENT

The documents that support risk management include:

Security Risk Factors	Archive-SRF	ISO 5.2.1
ISO 17799 certification	Archive-CE	ISO 5.2.2

5.2.1 THE REPOSITORY SHALL MAINTAIN A SYSTEMATIC ANALYSIS OF SECURITY RISK FACTORS ASSOCIATED WITH DATA, SYSTEMS, PERSONNEL, AND PHYSICAL PLANT

The risk factors associated with data, systems, personnel, and the physical plant are documented in the report, Archive-SRF. The report is generated externally, and is managed by Policy3-Policy8, Policy26, Policy35, and Policy36.

The Archive-SRF report is stored in GLOBAL_ACCOUNT/GLOBAL_REPOSITORY/GLOBAL_REPORTS.

The contents of the report include:

Operations – Mapping of ISO 27000 series of standards for controlling risk and threat to procedures

5.2.2 THE REPOSITORY SHALL HAVE IMPLEMENTED CONTROLS TO ADEQUATELY ADDRESS EACH OF THE DEFINED SECURITY RISKS

The controls for mitigating risk are also specified in the report, Archive-SRF. The controls include:

Physical security	card key access required to enter the facility
Passwords	all access requires authentication
Physical storage	all data are replicated across multiple storage systems
Personnel	roles are assigned to each staff member which enforces restrictions on allowed operations

Certification of the controls is documented in the report, Archive-CE. Compliance with ISO 17799 is required. The report is stored in GLOBAL_ACCOUNT/GLOBAL_REPOSITORY/GLOBAL_REPORTS. The report contains:

Operations – ISO 17799 Certificate

5.2.3 THE REPOSITORY STAFF SHALL HAVE DELINEATED ROLES, RESPONSIBILITIES, AND AUTHORIZATIONS RELATED TO IMPLEMENTING CHANGES WITHIN THE SYSTEM

The roles assigned to staff personnel are implemented in Policy9, rac-setRole.r. The allowed roles are:

Archive-manager	Has access to all reports
Archive-archivist	Has access to reports for an *Archive and can run *Archive-specific policies
Archive-admin	Has superuser access to the data grid, and can run policies that process all digital objects
Archive-IT	Has superuser access to the network and operating systems

Roles are verified by Policy10, rac-listRoles.r. This identifies the persons with each role. The results are documented in the report, Archive-SEA.

5.2.4 THE REPOSITORY SHALL HAVE SUITABLE WRITTEN DISASTER PREPAREDNESS AND RECOVERY PLAN(S), INCLUDING AT LEAST ONE OFF-SITE BACKUP OF ALL PRESERVED INFORMATION TOGETHER WITH AN OFF-SITE COPY OF THE RECOVERY PLAN(S)

A disaster recovery script archives all of the information and knowledge needed to recreate a data grid. The script archives sufficient information to enable the complete rebuilding of the repository on an entirely new hardware system. In effect, the information and knowledge needed to re-build the repository is archived, and used to re-instantiate the archive.

The script archives the information and knowledge that are needed for disaster recovery on an independent storage system, not used by the repository for preservation operations.

The Operations Plan document, Archive-OP, documents the disaster recovery procedure.

CHAPTER 6

Trustworthy Repository Implementation

The steps for designing a trustworthy repository were outlined in Section 1.1. The necessary design elements included:

- creation of management documents;

- specification of repository parameters;

- specification of preservation metadata attributes;

- specification of audit mechanisms to track all preservation actions;

- specification of policies that control operations performed upon the digital objects; and

- specification of infrastructure that manages technology evolution.

The DataNet Federation Consortium has implemented a trustworthy repository based on these necessary design elements. For each element, we list the tasks that need to be done, the ISO criterium driving the task, the name of the document that audits the task, and a policy that implements the task. There are several notable results.

- A policy may be used more than once, and may be used to support multiple ISO tasks.

- Three types of auditing mechanisms are used. Every action is logged in a manifest (log) file. Every report is versioned, enabling the tracking of both external management documents and internally generated output. An audit trail tracks every event. Comparisons between the manifest files and the audit trail can be used to identify events such as failed access attempts.

- Even though the 47 documents listed in Table 1.1 are generated externally to the repository, they still have to be managed, versioned, replicated, checksummed, and reviewed periodically. Ten policies manage these operations for the documents.

Table 6.1: Policies for managing externally generated documents

Task	Policy
Find the most recent version of a document	Policy4 – access the most recent version
Generate a new manifest file and version the old manifest	Policy55 – version all manifests and start new manifests
Generate checksum, version, replica, and set audit period for a document	Policy26 – checksum, version, replicate, and set audit period
Set attribute defining the name of an archive	Policy35 – set the name of an archives collection
Set default audit period for documents	Policy8 – set audit period for repository
Set the audit date for a document	Policy36 – set the audit date on a report
Set the audit date on all files in a collection	Policy80 – set the audit date on all files in a collection
Verify compliance with periodic audit	Policy3 – verify required update for a report
Verify existence of a document and list all versions	Policy5 – check existence and list versions
Verify status of all documents and generate report	Policy7 – analyze status of all reports, store result in Archive-SSA

Lists of the documents and policies for the additional design elements are given in the following tables.

Table 6.2: Procedures to set repository parameters

Task	ISO	Document	Policy
Register a policy	3.3.2	Archive-RAA	Policy16 – register a policy
Register an operation	3.3.2	Archive-RAA	Policy17 – register a micro-service
Set dates for completion of staff training	3.2.1.3	Archive-SEA	Policy11 – set date on staff member for training completion
Set public access to repository reports	3.3.4	Archive-RAA	Policy23 – set public access to repository reports
Set roles for staff	3.2.1.1	Archive-RAA	Policy9 – set the role of a staff member
Set the e-mail address for the repository administrator	4.1.7	Archive-RAA	Policy45 – set the e-mail address for the repository administrator
Set the events that are audited	3.3.3	Archive-RAA	Policy21 – set the events that are audited
Set training completion date for staff	3.2.1.3	Archive-SEA	Policy13 – save training completion information for a staff member

Table 6.3: Procedures to set preservation attributes

Task	ISO	Document	Policy
Retrieve a copy of the reserved vocabulary for an archive	4.2.7.2	Archive-HVOA	Policy78 – retrieve the reserved vocabulary from an external service
Set required metadata attributes on SIPS collection	4.1.5	Archive-PAA	Policy41 – set the required metadata attributes on SIPS collection
Set the e-mail address for the archivist	4.1.7	Archive-PAA	Policy44 – set the e-mail address for the archivist
Set the IPR owner attribute, Archive-IPR	3.5.2	Archive-IPA	Policy33 – register the IPR owner for a collection
Set the name of a designated community ontology	3.3.1	Archive-PAA	Policy14 – register the name of a community ontology
Set the name of the AIP template as attribute on the archive	4.2.1.1	Archive-PAA	Policy48 – set the AIP template name as attribute Archive-AIPTemplate
Set the source and depositor information	4.1.4	Archive-PAA	Policy39 – set the source and depositor information

Table 6.4: Procedures to audit all preservation actions

Task	ISO	Document	Policy
Log all preservation actions on SIPs	4.1.8	Archive-PAA	racWriteManifest policy function to record an action
Log notification of periodic reviews	3.1.2.2	Archive-NPRA	Policy6 – send e-mail yearly for review meetings, maintain a log of notifications
Notify archivist when required metadata is missing on a SIP	4.1.7	Archive-PAA	Policy47 – notify archivist where required metadata are missing on a SIP
Notify archivist when source and depositor are missing	4.1.7	Archive-PAA	Policy46 – notify archivist when provenance information is missing
Set auditing events	4.2.6.3	Audit trail	Policy62 – set audit policy for events related to SIPs, AIPs, DIPs

Task	ISO	Document	Policy
Verify a handle exists for each AIP	4.2.4	Archive-PAA	Policy57 – verify a handle exists for each AIP
Verify a SIP meets preservation requirements	4.2.2	Archive-PAA	Policy51 – verify a SIP satisfies preservation requirements
Verify access controls are compatible with IPR	3.5.2	Archive-IPA	Policy37 – verify access controls on an archive are compatible with IPR
Verify AIPs comply with preservation policies	4.2.2	Archive-AIP-CRA	Policy54 – verify each AIP complies with preservation requirements
Verify consistency of preservation operations	5.1.1.6	Archive-TRA	Policy76 – verify consistency between operations and state changes
Verify each SIP has required metadata	4.1.5	Archive-SIP-CRA	Policy43 – verify each SIP has required metadata
Verify existence of required replicas	3.3.5	Archive-RCA	Policy27 – verify required number of replicas exist
Verify file type conforms to required format for each AIP	4.3.2.1	Archive-PAA	Policy66 – verify that the format of each AIP conforms to required format types
Verify identifiers are preserved across operations	4.2.4.1.2	Archive-RAA	Policy58 – verify identifiers and metadata are preserved across repository operations
Verify integrity of all files in an archive	4.2.9	Archive-RCA	Policy64 – verify integrity of all files in an archive
Verify integrity of each AIP in an archive	3.3.5	Archive-RCA	Policy29 – verify integrity of each AIP and replace corrupted files
Verify repository documents have public access	3.3.4	Archive-RCA	Policy24 – analyze access permissions for repository reports
Verify required report updates are done	3.1	Archive-RAA	Policy3 – verify a required review has been completed on a report
Verify source and depositor are defined for each SIP	4.1.4	Archive-CINCA	Policy40 – verify provenance information set for each SIP

Task	ISO	Document	Policy
Verify status of all documents	3.1	Archive-SAA	Policy7 – analyze status of all reports
Verify that descriptive metadata is assigned to each AIP	4.5.2	Archive-MA	Policy79 – verify that descriptive information is assigned to every AIP
Verify that duplicate identifiers have not been made	4.2.4.2	Archive-IDCA	Policy59 – verify identifiers are not duplicated
Verify that the Archive-AIP-Template name is set	4.2.1.1	Archive-PAA	Policy49 – verify the Archive-AIPTemplate name is defined for an archive

Table 6.5: Procedures to implement preservation operations

Task	ISO	Document	Policy
Ensure information integrity	3.3.5	Audit trail	Policy26 – generate a checksum for all reports
Ensure replicas are synchronized	3.3.5	Archive-RAA	Policy28 – rebalance the replication resource to update replicas of changed files
Find an AIP from a description information term	4.5`	Archive-PAA	Policy70 – find an AIP from a term in Audit-Description
Find an AIP from its handle	4.5`	Archive-PAA	Policy69 – find an AIP from its handle
Find an AIP through a query on the descriptive metadata index	4.5`	Archive-PAA	Policy72 – find an AIPI from a query on an index of descriptive metadata
Generate a metadata file for each AIP	4.2.1.2	Archive-PAA	Policy50 – generate a metadata file (DIP) for each AIP
Generate a unique ID for each AIP	4.2.4	Archive-PAA	Policy56 – create a handle for an AIP
Generate AIPs from SIPs	4.2.2	Archive-AIP-CRA	Policy53 – generate an AIP for each SIP that has completed processing
Generate list of disputed data events	3.5.1.4	Archive-ALRA	Policy22 – generate a list of disputed data events

Task	ISO	Document	Policy
Generate staff experience report	3.2.1.2	Archive-SEA	Policy10 – list the number of staff in each role and their names in Archive-SEA.
Generate usage report	5.1.1.1.2	archive-URA	Policy75 – list usage (accesses, storage)
Identify all actions applied to an AIP	4.2.6	Archive-ARUA	Policy65 – list all actions applied to an AIP through query on audit trail
Identify all AIPs that need corrections	4.2.7.3	Archive-CINCA	Policy63 – list all AIPs that need corrections and notify archivist
Index the descriptive metadata	4.5	Archive-PAA	Policy71 – index the descriptive metadata terms, Audit-Description
List access events	4.6.1	Archive-ALA	Policy73 – get all access events
List access failure events	4.6.1.1	Archive-AFA	Policy74 – get all access failure event
List all users who have access	3.5.1.4	Archive-ALRA	Policy32 – list the users who have access
List archive contents	4.1.1.2	Archive-CIRA	Policy38 – list the archive contents and file types
List status of all SIPs	4.2.2	Archive-SAPA	Policy52 – list status of all SIPs to verify process completion
List the AIPs in an archive and their creation dates	4.1.6	Archive-ARA	Policy77 – list the AIPs and their creation dates
List the names of community ontologies	3.3.1	Archive-RAA	Policy15 – list the designated community ontology for all archives
List the policies that are in use	3.3.2	Archive-PPA	Policy25 – list the policies that are in the rule base
List the preservation properties that are in use	3.3.2	Archive-PMRA	Policy20 – list the preservation attributes in use in the Archive
List training completion dates for staff	3.2.1.3	Archive-SEA	Policy12 – list completed training for each staff member

Task	ISO	Document	Policy
Remove access to by a specified account	3.5.1.4	Archive-ALRA	Policy30 – remove access for a specified user
Remove non-compatible access based on IPR	3.5.2	Archive-IPA	Policy34 – remove non-compliant access controls for compatibility with IPR
Set access for a specified account	3.5.1.4	Archive-ALRA	Policy31 – set access for s specified user
Set required metadata on a SIP	4.1.5	Archive-SIP-CRA	Policy42 – set SIP metadata
Set the format type for an AIP	4.2.5.1	Archive-PAA	Policy60 – set the file type of an AIP
Transform the format of an AIP	4.2.5.2	Archive-PAA	Policy61 – invoke an external service to identify or transform an AIP

Table 6.6: Procedures to manage infrastructure

Task	ISO	Document	Policy
List all of the infrastructure components	5.1.1.1.1	Archive-ILA	izoneReport – list all software and hardware components of the data grid
List the format transformations that can be applied to AIPs	4.4.1	Archive-DIRA	Policy68 – retrieve the supported format transformations from an external service
List the infrastructure components that were used	3.3.3	Archive-IRA	Policy81 – list the infrastructure components used for preservation
List the service components provided by the repository	4.2.5	Archive-DIRA	Policy67 – list the services invoked by preservation procedures
Maintain bi-directional links to metadata	4.5.3	Audit trail	acSetVaultPathPolicy
Manage disaster recovery	5.2.4	Archive-RAA	disasterRecovery.sh script
Monitor usage to decide when technology changes are needed	5.1.1.1.2	Archive-URA	Policy75 – generate usage report for technology components

CHAPTER 7

Summary

The policies listed in Tables 6.1–6.6 constitute a set of computer actionable rules that enforce the ISO 16363 Trustworthiness Assessment criteria. These rules are based on the Global Parameters defined in Table 2.1 that specify the structure of the repository. The preservation attributes that are managed by the repository are defined in Table 2.2. The reports that document compliance with the ISO 16363 criteria are listed in Table 2.3.

The combination of repository parameters, preservation attributes, audit reports, and preservation policies constitute a complete design proscription for the implementation of a trusted digital repository.

The applicability of the ISO 16363 criteria to community specific data management plans is illustrated by the mapping of the National Science Foundation data management plan requirements to criteria defined by ISO 16363. The NSF data management plan requirements are a subset of the requirements specified by the ISO standard.

References

1. Audit and Certification of Trustworthy Digital Repositories. Recommended Practice. 2011 CCSDS http://public.ccsds.org/publications/archive/652x0m1.pdf. xiii

2. Audit Preparation and Self-Assessment Template for ISO 16363. 2013 PTAB http://www.iso16363.org/preparing-for-an-audit/. xiii

3. Chen, S.-Y., M. Conway, J. Crabtree, C. Lee, S. Misra, R. Moore, A. Rajasekar, T. Russell, I. Simmons, L. Stillwell, H. Tibbo, H. Xu, "Policy Templates Workbook – iRODS 4.0", iRODS Consortium. xiii

4. Chen, S.-Y., M. Conway, J. Crabtree, C. Lee, S. Misra, R. Moore, A. Rajasekar, T. Russell, I. Simmons, L. Stillwell, H. Tibbo, H. Xu, "Policy Examples Workbook – iRODS 4.0", iRODS Consortium. 7

5. Moore, R. A. Rajasekar, H. Xu, "DataNet Federation Consortium Policy Toolkits", iPRES conference, November 2015. 7

6. Moore, R., R. Stotzka, C. Cacciari, P. Benedikt, "Practical Policy Templates", Research Data Alliance Practical Policy Working Group, February, 2015, DOI: 10.15497/83E1B3F9-7E17-484A-A466-B3E5775121CC. 7

7. Moore, R., R. Stotzka, C. Cacciari, P. Benedikt, "Practical Policy Implementations", Rescarch Data Alliance a Practical Policy Working Group, February, 2015, DOI: 10.15497/83E1B3F9-7E17-484A-A466-B3E5775121CC. 7

8. Moore, R. W., Rajasekar, A., Wan, M. (2010). IRODS policy sets as standards for preservation. Roadmap for Digital Preservation Interoperability Framework Workshop, US-DPIF'10. (December 01, 2010). ACM International Conference Proceeding Series. DOI: 10.1145/2039274.2039283. 7

9. Moore, R., "Towards a Theory of Digital Preservation", IJDC Volume 3, Issue 1, pp 63–75, August 2008. 7

10. Moore, R., M. Smith, "Automated Validation of Trusted Digital Repository Assessment Criteria", Journal of Digital Information, Vol 8, No 2 (2007). 7

11. Moore, R., "Building Preservation Environments with Data Grid Technology", American Archivist, vol. 69, no. 1, pp. 139–158, July 2006. 7

12.   Moore, R., M. Smith, "Assessment of RLG Trusted Digital Repository Requirements," JCDL on "Digital Curation & Trusted Repositories: Seeking Success", June 2006, Chapel Hill, North Carolina. xiii

13.   Rajasekar, A., T. Russell, J. Coposky, A. de Torcy, H. Xu, M. Wan, R. Moore, W. Schroeder, S-Y Chen, M. Conway, J. Ward, "The integrated Rule-Oriented Data Systems (iRODS 4.0) Micro-service Workbook", iRODS Consortium. 7

14.   Rajasekar, R., M. Wan, R. Moore, W. Schroeder, S.-Y. Chen, L. Gilbert, C.-Y. Hou, C. Lee, R. Marciano, P. Tooby, A. de Torcy, B. Zhu, "iRODS Primer: Integrated Rule-Oriented Data System", Morgan & Claypool, 2010. 7

15.   Rajasekar, A., M. Wan, R. Moore, W. Schroeder, "A Prototype Rule-based Distributed Data Management System", HPDC workshop on "Next Generation Distributed Data Management", May 2006, Paris, France. 7

16.   Reference Model for an Open Archival Information System (OAIS). 2012 CCSDS http://public.ccsds.org/publications/archive/650x0m2.pdf. xiii

17.   Requirements for Bodies Providing Audit and Certification of Candidate Trustworthy Digital Repositories. 2014 CCSDS http://public.ccsds.org/publications/archive/652x1m2.pdf. xiii

18.   Smith, M., R. Moore, "Digital Archive Policies and Trusted Digital Repositories", proceedings of The 2nd International Digital Curation Conference: Digital Data Curation in Practice, November 2006, Glasgow, Scotland, IJDC 2(1): pp 92-101, 2007. DOI: 10.2218/ijdc.v2i1.16. xiii

19.   Sproull, Robert, J. Eisenberg, Editors: Committee on Digital Archiving and the National Archives and Records Administration: National Research Council, DOI: 10.17226/10707. xiii

20.   Trusted Digital Repositories: Attributes and Responsibilities, an RLG-OCLC Report, http://www.oclc.org/content/dam/research/activities/trustedrep/repositories.pdf. xiii

21.   Trustworthy Repositories Audit & Certification: Criteria and Checklist. 2007 CRL http://www.crl.edu/sites/default/files/d6/attachments/pages/trac_0.pdf. xiii

22.   Ward, J., M. Wan, W. Schroeder, A. Rajasekar, A. de Torcy, T. Russell, H. Xu, R. Moore, "The integrated Rule-Oriented Data System (iRODS 3.0) Micro-service Workbook", DICE Foundation, November 2011, ISBN: 9781466469129, Amazon.com. 7

Author Biographies

Dr. Reagan W. Moore is a professor in the School of Information and Library Science at the University of North Carolina, Chapel Hill, chief scientist for Data Intensive Cyber Environments at the Renaissance Computing Institute, and director of the Data Intensive Cyber Environments Center at University of North Carolina (UNC-CH). He coordinates research efforts in the development of data grids, digital libraries, and preservation environments. Developed software systems include the Storage Resource Broker data grid and the integrated Rule-Oriented Data System. Supported projects include the National Archives and Records Administration Transcontinental Persistent Archive Prototype and the science data grids for seismology, oceanography, climate, high-energy physics, astronomy, and bioinformatics. An ongoing research interest is the use of data-grid technology to automate the execution of management policies and validate the trustworthiness of repositories. Dr. Moore's previous roles include the following: director of the DICE group at the San Diego Supercomputer Center; and Manager of production services at SDSC. He previously worked as a computational plasma physicist, at General Atomics on equilibrium and stability of toroidal fusion devices. He has a Ph.D. in plasma physics from the University of California, San Diego (1978), and a B.S. in physics from the California Institute of Technology (1967).

Dr. Arcot Rajasekar is a professor in the School of Library and Information Science at the University of North Carolina, Chapel Hill (UNC-CH), and a chief scientist at the Renaissance Computing Institute (RENCI). Previously, he was at the San Diego Supercomputer Center at the University of California, San Diego, leading the Data Grids Technology Group. He has been involved in research and development of data grid middleware systems for over a decade and is a lead originator behind the concepts in the Storage Resource Broker (SRB) and the integrated Rule-Oriented Data Systems (iRODS), two premier data grid middleware systems developed by the Data Intensive Cyber Environments Group. Dr. Rajasekar has a Ph.D. in computer science from the University of Maryland at College Park and has more than 100 publications in the areas of data grids, logic programming, deductive databases, digital library, and persistent archives.

Dr. Hao Xu is a research scientist at the Data Intensive CyberEnvironment Center, University of North Carolina at Chapel Hill (UNC-CH). He has been working on improving the rule engine and the rule language, and the metadata catalog of the integrated Rule-Oriented Data System (iRODS) since 2010. He developed the pluggable rule engine architecture that allows interoperability between different programming languages and the iRODS data management systems. He also developed QueryArrow, a semantically unified query engine that allows bidirectional integration of metadata from multiple heterogeneous metadata sources. His research interests include the theory of data management, automatic theorem proving, programming languages, distributed data systems, and formal methods in software development. He has a B.E. in Computer Science and Engineering and a B.S. minor in Applied Mathematics from Beihang University, and a Ph.D in Compuer Science from UNC-CH.

Jonathan Crabtree is Assistant Director for Cyberinfrastructure at the Odum Institute for Research in Social Science at the University of North Carolina at Chapel Hill (UNC-CH). As assistant director, Crabtree completely revamped the institute's technology infrastructure and has positioned the institute to assume a leading national role in information archiving. He is co-designer of the Virtual Institute for Social Research (VISR) and its integration into the research data lifecycle. He is currently enrolled in the UNC School of Information and Library Science doctoral program with his area of interest focused on the auditing of trusted repositories.

Mike Conway is a software developer with over 20 years experience in distributed systems development. Mike is currently finishing up his master's degree in Information Science at the School of Information and Library Science at the University of North Carolina at Chapel Hill (UNC-CH). Most recently, Mike has been an architect and developer on the iRODS data grid, as well as the DataNet Federation Consortium, developing interfaces and protocols to support distributed, policy-managed environments in support of scientific research and digital preservation. Mike is also a developer with the iRODS Consoritum, based at the Renaissance Computing Institute (RENCI) at UNC-CH, contributing to the continued development of the iRODS open source data grid. Mike has also contributed to research in the areas of metadata management, applied cyberinfrastructure, and trusted digitial preservation environments.

Dr. Helen R. Tibbo is an Alumni Distinguished Professor at the School of Information and Library Science (SILS) at the University of North Carolina at Chapel Hill (UNC-CH), and teaches in the areas of archives and records management, digital preservation and access, appraisal, trustworthy repositories, and data curation. She developed the Archives and Records Management (ARM) Program at SILS and teaches in the SILS Post Master's Certificate in Data Curation. She is also the Director of a soon-to-be-offered Master's in Professional Science in Digital Curation degree program. She is also a Fellow of the Society of American Archivists (SAA) and was SAA President 2010–2011.

From 2006-2009, Dr. Tibbo was the Principal Investigator (PI) for the IMLS (Institute for Museum and Library Services)-funded DigCCurr I project that developed an International Digital Curation Curriculum for master's level students (www.ils.unc.edu/digccurr). She was also the PI for DigCCurr II (2008–2013) that extended the Digital Curation Curriculum to the doctoral level. In 2009, IMLS awarded Prof. Tibbo two additional projects, Educating Stewards of Public Information in the 21st Century (ESOPI-21) and Closing the Digital Curation Gap (CDCG). In 2011, IMLS awarded Dr. Tibbo funding for the Educating Stewards of the Public Information Infrastructure (ESOPI2) project that is continuing the work of ESOPI-21 through 2015. In

April 2013, Dr. Tibbo received an IMLS award for the "Curating Research Assets and Data using Lifecycle Education: Data Management Education Tools for Librarians, Archivists, and Content Creators or CRADLE project.

Dr. Tibbo is the head of the Standards and Policies Community of Practice for the DataNet Federation Consortium and was also a co-PI with collaborators from the University of Michigan and the University of Toronto on a National Historical Publications and Records Commission (NHPRC)-funded project to develop standardized metrics for assessing use and user services for primary sources in government settings. Dr. Tibbo was part of the original Library of Congress Digital Preservation Outreach and Education Train-the-Trainer instructional team in September 2011. She also conducted test ISO 16363 audits of repositories in Europe and the U.S. during the summer of 2011 and is a founding member of the Primary Trustworthy Digital Repository Audit and Certification Board (PTAB). She was also a member of the DigCurV project team funded by the European Commission's Leonardo DaVinci Program.